We dedicate this book to our mothers
who taught us a love for good food,
its preparation and presentation.

Tide's Table

MARITIME COOKING
from **INN ON THE COVE**

ROSS & WILLA MAVIS

GOOSE LANE EDITIONS

Published by Goose Lane Editions with the assistance of the Department of Canadian Heritage and the New Brunswick Department of Municipalities, Culture and Housing.

Cover photo by David Corkum, Hawk Communications Inc.
Illustrations © Lynn Wigginton, 1996. Reproduced with permission.
Back cover photo by Flewwelling Photography.
Edited by Charles Stuart, Susanne Alexander and Julie Watson.
Book design by Darren Lee, Lee~Current Design.
Printed in Canada by Gagné Printing.
  10 9 8 7 6 5 4 3

Canadian Cataloguing in Publication Data

Mavis, Ross, 1941-

  Tide's table

  Includes index.
  ISBN 0-86492-208-6 (PB)
  ISBN 0-86492-216-7 (HC)

1. Cookery, Canadian — Maritime style.   I. Mavis, Willa, 1945-
II. Title.

TX15.6.M38   641.59715   C96-950151-X

Goose Lane Editions
469 King Street
Fredericton, New Brunswick
CANADA E3B 1E5

Contents

ACKNOWLEDGMENTS

Over twenty years ago, on both coasts of Canada, two people who love to cook were hoping to write a cookbook one day. In fact, they also had a vision of a television cooking show. Grandiose ideas perhaps for an individual, but attainable for two like-minded people.

When we met in 1985, we quickly discovered we shared many of the same dreams. Operating an inn was another aspiration and the first we fulfilled. Inn on the Cove had its grand opening on April 30, 1992. Our friends Bea and John gave us a card of congratulations which read "Success comes to those who take a dream and make it come true." We must thank them for helping us make that dream a reality.

In February 1993, we taped the first two episodes of *Tide's Table* in the kitchen of our Inn. The folks at Fundy Cable held our hands through the next fifty-two shows and continue to support us in our efforts.

In August 1994, we began discussions with Laurel Boone at Goose Lane Editions about publishing a cookbook. Laurel wrote to us on September 13th asking for a sample chapter. She encouraged us by saying our recipes seemed "instructive as well as entertaining" and went on to say she thought "it would be fun to work" with us. Laurel's attention was demanded on another project, and we were introduced to Susanne Alexander who has guided us through the maze of recipes and ideas to where we are today. And Laurel was right, it has been fun. But why wouldn't it be, we're both doing what we enjoy most, messing about with food, and we're doing it together.

It's a great luxury working on a project with your spouse, and it certainly wouldn't be possible to walk away from the obligations of running our Inn if it wasn't for our assistant, Marilyn Abric. She and the other members of our staff have often kept the guests happy and well fed while we sat at our computers. She also has willingly sampled many of our recipes and cleaned the pots and bowls resulting from our experiments.

Our home-away-from-home is the Saint John City Market and the shoppers and merchants always ask "What's cooking today?" as we shop up and down the aisles. We appreciate the products supplied to us for our TV show and this cookbook by many of the businesses in the market, in particular, Lord's Lobsters, Perry's Meats and Pete's Frootique.

Many recipes from Willa's family were compiled in a well-worn notebook given to Willa by her sister Roberta over thirty years ago. Handwritten additions from other family members, including Ross's family, have been added over the years, and it's good to know they will live on for generations to come.

We wish to thank guests, family and friends for the many recipes given to us when they heard about our book. Some of them have found their way in this, our first, cookbook; others will be saved for the next one. The folks at Goose Lane have been patient and understanding and found the very best people to work with us. We especially wish to thank Julie Watson and Charles Stuart, who kept us on our toes, Lynn Wigginton, who provided the beautiful drawings for the book and David Corkum and Martin Flewwelling, our two photographers, for making our food and ourselves look so good.

Finally, a sincere thanks to our families, staff and friends, who have lent us support and encouragement.

Ross and Willa Mavis

10

$\mathcal{I}$think I have always been a "good cook" in most things I've done. Seldom have I been intimidated by a task, no matter how challenging it might have seemed at first. That doesn't mean I have always been successful at everything I've set my hand to, but my wins have outnumbered my losses.

Cooking requires some knowledge, but it demands much more in the way of imagination, courage and the desire to get it right. Good cooks make good inn-keepers because both must have an overriding love for people. It is this desire to please and satisfy your family, friends and guests that allows you to shine as cook and innkeeper. Willa has often told me that I'm happiest when I'm in the kitchen cooking. She, I believe, is happiest when she is engaged in conversation with our guests. What a team!

I have always been quick to start preparing food at the slightest hint that company might be coming. Even as a young person, when I didn't want to go on a Sunday outing with my mother and father, I couldn't wait for them to leave the house so I could start whipping up something for supper. Good cooks are either self-taught, trained by skilled chefs or born with an instinct for food preparation. I have never had any formal cooking training and therefore admit to being a self-taught and instinctive cook.

I value my cooking instinct as much as any self-training. Instinctive cooks can read recipes and taste in their imagination how each ingredient affects the over-all taste of the dish. I read a recipe and immediately start adjusting it to suit my own tastes. It's important that novice and accomplished cooks alike realize that recipes should only be considered guidelines. Truly inspired cooking occurs like great art — when you allow yourself to colour outside the lines. If I have influenced my wife's cooking at all during the years we have been together, it has been to give her the courage to try something different in her recipes. Not that she always agrees the change is better, necessary or warranted — but the important thing is that she has had the courage to try something different.

When it comes to new foods, we have also encouraged our children to at least experiment. During her formative years, our daughter Morgan grew to like broccoli, parsnips, squash and spinach — no small success for a child. She still doesn't like raw oysters, but at least has the courage to try them once a year to see if her tastes have changed.

I exhort our readers to exercise courage in their cooking. Let your cuisine reflect your personality and outlook. Use recipes as a general floor plan, but decide yourself where your windows and doors are to go. It is only through courageous experimentation and keen imagination that truly great cooks develop.

From the title and opening shot to the closing toast on each show, I've had the *Tide's Table* cooking show clearly in my head for twenty years. (A book usually inspires a TV series, but wouldn't you know we would do it in reverse.) It all developed from the saying of my good friend Tex Lyon in Port Hardy, British Columbia: "When the tide is low, the table is set." I imagined crystal goblets gleaming alongside silver cutlery; a fine china place setting carefully laid on rough driftwood timbers awash with the incoming tide. This vision became *Tide's Table*.

The sea has always been an overwhelming influence in my life. The wild and treacherous waters of Queen Charlotte Strait in British Columbia and the Bay of Fundy's tremendous tides in New Brunswick both lured me to their shores. ["Actually, it was I who lured him to the New Brunswick shores." — Willa] I have always loved the fruits of the sea, and salmon and cod, halibut and mackerel, lobster, oysters, clams and mussels have fed families on both coasts of Canada since time immemorial. The abundance of marine life in our oceans has nourished the very roots of our Canadian heritage. And it is for this reason that *Tide's Table* is dedicated to all Maritime cooking — not just Maritime seafood, but also the recipes of Maritime seafarers.

You cannot discuss seafood and the Martimes without mentioning lobster. This highly prized, regal crustacean was once considered the fare of poor fisher folk. A few decades ago, many a Maritime school child was ashamed to admit their sandwiches contained lobster. But times, attitudes and prices have changed. Lobster is now king, and the Maritimes its kingdom.

With rapidly decreasing fish stocks throughout the world, however, it behoves cooks to broaden their vision to include the landlubber's larder. Happily, we in the Maritimes are blessed with an abundant variety of other foods. Maritime soils produce fruits and vegetables second to none. We're well known for indigenous natural products such as cranberries, blueberries, mushrooms, honey, maple syrup, wild rice and fiddlehead ferns, to name just a few. Even more food abounds from the diligence and labour of our farmers and fishers. We can thank them for the availability of domestic fruits, vegetables, meat, poultry, dairy and seafood.

There has also been a recent explosion of growth in small-scale, niche-market speciality food producers. Domestic Cheddar and low-fat cheeses, unique Gouda and quark, herb and vegetable spreads, maple sugar and candies, apple ciders and vinegars, smoked meats and fancy sausages, apple and maple liqueurs, smoked salmon and oysters, pickles and sauerkraut, organic whole grain flours and cereals, Arctic char and rainbow trout, pheasants and game hens — these plus many other home-produced food products now come daily to our market.

Any credible guide to Maritime cooking must be sure to touch on the full spectrum of this rainbow of culinary colours. This is exactly the task that we embraced: to produce a book that does justice to the range and splendour of Maritime foods. These dishes are designed to give you a full Maritime culinary sensation, and maybe even to challenge your tastebuds. They are also meant to be delicious to eat and fun to make. I'll go out on a limb and promise you pleasure in the making and the eating. No doubt Willa has some promises of her own that you won't want to miss, so let's get in the kitchen and get cooking!

— *Ross*

*I*sn't that just like Ross. He's told his story, come home from the supermarket loaded with groceries and wants us all to join him in the kitchen — right now! Just a second, Ross. Don't forget the first thing you do here in the Maritimes when you get home from town. Yes, dear, even before you bring in the twenty-one bags of perishables. That's right, you put on the kettle for a nice cup of tea.

Ross and I met eleven years ago, and it's taken me all that time to slow him down a bit — to take the time to smell the chow chow simmering on the back of the stove, as it were. He's coming along nicely. He now prefers tea to coffee and puts the milk in his cup first. He admits publicly that our wild-grown blueberries are superior to the "all show, no flavour" cultivated ones he was accustomed to out West. Even his mother admits preferring haddock to Pacific cod. (We uprooted her at the age of eighty-four from the north end of Vancouver Island and settled her here on the Fundy Shore where she's become an honorary Maritimer.)

Anyway, as I was saying, Ross and I met eleven years ago in the Romance Capital of Canada — Toronto. We even lived there for several years. But, like they say, "You can take a Maritimer out of the Maritimes, but you can't take the Maritimes out of a Maritimer." (Don't quote me on that, I generally get those clever expressions wrong.) Back we came to the banks of the beautiful St. John River, and it's been great ever since.

We have a summer house on the river, right next door to the house where I grew up. I'm the youngest of eight — not an easy position in a family that is not well off. But our family was rich beyond compare for the wonderful meals my Mum prepared so lovingly. Mum was my best friend when I was growing up, so I spent a lot of time with her in the kitchen and pantry. That's where I developed my love of cooking. She used her culinary skills to win the hearts of everyone who walked through the kitchen door. Telephone men, linemen, metermen, mailmen, milkmen and their wives came back summer after summer to sample Mum's cooking. And Dad would sit in his captain's chair in the corner of the kitchen and beam as everyone asked for seconds.

As a kid, I played hostess when Mum and Dad had family friends Dottie and Les in for the evening. I prepared fancy sandwiches decorated with pickles and carrot sticks. I'd arrange the sweets in a stylish order and make tea, serving it in our best china cups. Little did I know I was preparing myself for being an innkeeper.

Mum used to say, "You attract more bees with honey than you do with vinegar." I soon found that by cooking on Saturdays, I was the centre of attention on Saturday nights. My three brothers and my dad would rave about my cinnamon pinwheel biscuits (learned in home economics at Saint John Vocational School).

Running an inn is a lot like caring for a big family. You have to be the first one up in the morning and make sure the tables are set, muffins in the oven and coffee brewing, all before you have your tea and toast. A lot of guests, many of them businessmen and women, come back every month. We know all about their families, but most importantly, what they like and don't like to eat. Who likes herbal tea, and what kind; who wants toast, no butter, and marmalade; and who wants a full-cooked breakfast, but no fruit on the plate. The dinners can be gruelling. We once did a sit-down dinner for fifty-six people just using our four-burner stove!

We have to get along well, if we're going to work in the kitchen together. We cook in the same room we serve our meals in, so we have to be on our best behaviour. We handle it well. Ross does most of the meat and fish dishes, I prepare most of the vegetables and salads. We share soups, appetizers and desserts, although Ross makes the sorbets and does the food presentation. Often guests lean their elbows on the edge of the counter and discuss the meal we're preparing for them. This was a little off-putting at first, although it reminded me of my mother's kitchen, but now we chat away while stirring, chopping and peeling. And we both delight in the comments we hear from guests who appreciate fine food and good service.

When Ross and I met, the first thing that struck me about him was his sense of humour. They say that is what a woman really wants in a man. Well, I had a double bonus because at the age of thirty-nine I not only found one of the funniest guys of all time, but a man who loved to cook. It was like having a high score on *Wheel of Fortune* and going on to win the bonus round! ["Hold it, Willa. I think I object to being called the bonus round."— Ross]

Ours has definitely been a marriage made in the kitchen. So, like Ross said, "Why don't you open this book and join us there?"

— *Willa*

15

A Note on Herbs

We prefer to use fresh herbs for cooking. However, we are completely at home using dried herbs as well. Quantities given in these recipes are usually for dried herbs unless otherwise noted. Should fresh herbs be available, follow our rule of thumb by substituting 1 tsp of dried herbs with 1 Tbsp of fresh herbs.

— W & R

BOUNTIFUL BEGINNINGS

Breakfasts . . .
a Specialty
of the House

1 Tbsp	BUTTER OR VEGETABLE OIL	15 ml
6	EGGS	6
⅓ cup	MILK OR 10% CREAM	75 ml
	SALT AND PEPPER TO TASTE	
½ cup	FRESH PARSLEY, FINELY CHOPPED	125 ml
½ cup	CHEDDAR CHEESE, GRATED	125 ml
	PARSLEY AND CHERRY TOMATOES FOR GARNISHING	

Heat butter in a non-stick frying pan over medium heat; break in eggs one at a time. Cook until whites are just beginning to set; spoon milk onto eggs and stir lightly, taking care to leave a definition between the whites and the yolks. Season with salt and pepper. Gently mix, lifting the cooked eggs from the bottom of the pan. Sprinkle with parsley. Add grated cheese and cover. Cook for about 2 minutes, until cheese melts. Cut into four wedges and serve on warmed plates with parsley and cherry tomatoes for garnish.

SERVES 4.

HERB & CHEESE EGGS

We had prepared breakfasts for dozens of friends and family members before we became innkeepers. However, we weren't prepared for the morning our first guests came down for breakfast. The pressure was on; this meal was going to be critiqued by paying people from away. Our herb and cheese eggs won them over, we're happy to say. One guest said, "These are the best eggs I've ever eaten in my life!" Whew, we'd done it. We were officially innkeepers.

W & R

19
BOUNTIFUL BEGINNINGS

TIP: *You can substitute any combination of herbs for the parsley. We've also used chives, basil, paprika and tarragon.*

Heggs & Salmon

One of the first recipes we prepared for visiting family members when we lived in Toronto was this dish of eggs, salmon and hollandaise on buttermilk biscuits. Willa's sister, Roberta, was impressed with the quick and easy hollandaise sauce we whipped up in the microwave. Her husband loved how the lemony sauce and egg yolk complemented the smoked salmon. It was a great recipe for us to make because our kitchen was so small. We had a toaster oven, hot plate and microwave, but no conventional stove.

R

BISCUIT BASE

3 CUPS	FLOUR	750 ML
1 TSP	SALT	5 ML
1 ½ TSP	BAKING SODA	7 ML
1 TBSP	CREAM OF TARTAR	15 ML
1 TSP	BAKING POWDER	5 ML
½ CUP	BUTTER	125 ML
1 ⅓ CUPS	BUTTERMILK	325 ML

TOPPING

12	THIN SLICES SMOKED SALMON	12
12	EGGS, POACHED OR SCRAMBLED	12
	HOLLANDAISE SAUCE	
	FRESH DILL, PAPRIKA, CHERRY TOMATOES	
	AND ZUCCHINI SLICES FOR GARNISHING	

PREHEAT OVEN TO 375° F / 190° C.

Mix dry ingredients in a large bowl; cut in butter with a pastry blender or two knives. Add buttermilk and stir until well combined. Gather into a ball and place on a lightly floured surface. Knead 8 or 10 times and pat or roll dough to a thickness of ¾ inch / 2 cm; cut with large (4 inch / 10 cm) biscuit cutter. Place on a baking sheet and brush tops of biscuits with milk. Bake 10 to 12 minutes until golden brown.

Split biscuits in half and cover with a thin slice of smoked salmon. Poach or scramble eggs (allowing 2 eggs per person) and place on top of smoked salmon. Drizzle with **Thick and Easy Hollandaise Sauce.** Garnish with fresh dill and a pinch of paprika. Serve two halves with cherry tomatoes and zucchini slices for accent.

SERVES 6.

Eggs in Kilts

6 OR 8	EGGS, HARD BOILED	6 OR 8
1 LB	SPICY SAUSAGE MEAT	450 G
½ TSP	THYME	2 ML
½ TSP	BASIL	2 ML
	SALT AND PEPPER TO TASTE	
¼ CUP	FLOUR	50 ML
1 CUP	BREADCRUMBS	250 ML
1 TSP	PEPPER	5 ML
1 TSP	PAPRIKA	5 ML
¼ CUP	FLOUR	50 ML
2	EGGS, WELL BEATEN	2
	OIL FOR FRYING	

My Scottish lineage bubbles to the surface every now and then with a recipe adapted from the ones my dear old Mum handed down to me. Eggs in Kilts, as I affectionately refer to them, are a treat for all occasions, whether a summer picnic or a fall brunch. They are not only "neat looking," but also a handy way to make a breakfast of sausage and eggs.

R

Carefully peel hard-boiled eggs and refrigerate until needed. Mix sausage meat in a small bowl with spices, salt and pepper. Dry eggs and roll them in flour to lightly coat them. Mix breadcrumbs with pepper and paprika and set aside. Divide sausage mixture into portions equal to the number of eggs. Shape sausage mixture around each egg, carefully enclosing it inside. Roll sausage-covered eggs in flour, then in beaten egg, and finally in reserved breadcrumb mixture. Deep-fry coated eggs in hot oil until they are well browned. (You can use a regular frying pan and less oil, but you must constantly turn the eggs to brown them completely and equally.) Drain on paper towel and cool before serving. Cut eggs in half lengthwise to reveal what's under the kilt and serve with a dab of hot mustard.

SERVES 4 TO 6.

Scrambled Eggs Vol-au-Vent

Operating a bed & breakfast style country inn, we're constantly looking for new breakfast recipes, not because our guests tire of our omelettes and pancakes but because after cooking breakfast seven days a week for four years, we need something different. Yes, it's scrambled eggs, but what an elegant presentation. This makes an impressive Sunday brunch too.

W&R

8	PATTY SHELLS, HEATED	8
2 TBSP	BUTTER OR MARGARINE	30 ML
12	EGGS, BEATEN	12
2/3 CUP	MILK	150 ML
2 TBSP	FRESH CHIVES, CHOPPED	30 ML
	SALT AND PEPPER TO TASTE	
8 OZ	CREAM CHEESE, CUBED	225 G
4	SLICES BACON, COOKED	4
	CHERRY TOMATOES AND FRESH PARSLEY FOR GARNISHING	

Melt butter in a large non-stick frying pan. Combine eggs, milk, chives and seasonings in a separate bowl. Pour into pan and stir constantly over low-medium heat until eggs begin to set; add cream cheese, stirring occasionally until cheese is blended and eggs are cooked.

Serve in patty shells. Cut each bacon slice in half, roll up and place on top of eggs. Decorate plate with cherry tomato halves and fresh parsley sprigs.

SERVES 8.

TIP: *If patty shells are unavailable, use croissants. Cut each croissant in half, leaving the top and bottom attached. Fill with scrambled eggs and serve with bacon or sausage on the side.*

6	SLICES STALE BREAD, CUT IN STRIPS	6
1 TBSP	BUTTER	15 ML
¼ CUP	ONION, CHOPPED	50 ML
4	SLICES BACON, CRISPLY FRIED	4
¼ CUP	CHEDDAR CHEESE, GRATED	50 ML
2 TBSP	TOMATO SAUCE	30 ML
4	EGGS, SLIGHTLY BEATEN	4
	SALT AND PEPPER TO TASTE	
4 CUPS	MILK	1 L

PREHEAT OVEN TO 375° F / 180° C.

*L*ightly grease a 9 x 9-inch / 2.5-litre casserole. Lay half the bread strips in the bottom of the casserole. Melt the butter in a frying pan and sauté the onion until it is soft and transparent. Break crisply fried bacon into bits. Sprinkle bacon, onion and cheese over bread in casserole. Dot with tomato sauce. Cover with remaining bread strips. Lightly beat eggs, adding salt and pepper to taste. Bring milk close to boiling in a saucepan over medium heat, or in a Pyrex dish in the microwave; quickly beat in eggs, and pour over bread. Let sit for 15 to 20 minutes. Set dish in pan of hot water and bake in oven for 35 to 45 minutes. Cool 5 minutes; cut in quarters and serve.

SERVES 4.

*B*REAKFAST *P*UDDING

This is a great recipe to make when you have leftovers or not quite enough of anything for a traditional breakfast. It uses stale bread, requires only one strip of bacon and one egg per person, and makes use of that little end of cheese. Put them all together with some tomato sauce (we've even used ketchup or salsa) and you have a delicious breakfast. Garnish the plate with some fresh fruit slices or a baked tomato half and parsley. Your guests will be so impressed that they won't know they're eating leftovers.

W & R

23
BOUNTIFUL
BEGINNINGS

Buttermilk Pancakes

Pancakes were a mainstay of the winter breakfasts of my childhood. Mum cooked her pancakes on a large, round griddle greased with a rag she kept in a cup of bacon fat. The night before, she would prepare the batter in a wonderful old stone pitcher. Just before breakfast, she would mix a bit of baking soda with water and pour it into the batter, filling our kitchen with the aroma of fresh pancake batter. Pancakes were usually accompanied by a bowl of hot oatmeal porridge, pork scraps or sausage patties and tea. Today, we like to serve pancakes with bacon or sausage and fresh fruit.

W

TIP: *To test for the proper heat of a griddle, sprinkle a drop of water on the hot surface: if it dances and sizzles, the griddle is hot enough. Once the pancake starts to cook, lower the temperature.*

2 CUPS	WHITE OR WHOLE WHEAT FLOUR OR A BLEND OF BOTH	500 ML
1 TSP	BAKING SODA	5 ML
1 TSP	SALT	5 ML
2 CUPS	BUTTERMILK	500 ML
3	EGGS, BEATEN	3
¼ CUP	VEGETABLE OIL OR MELTED BUTTER	50 ML

Sift dry ingredients together in a large bowl. Stir in buttermilk, eggs and oil; beat well, but not until smooth. Pancakes are lighter if some lumps remain in batter.

Fry on a lightly greased, heated griddle or frying pan over medium heat until edges of pancake begin to dry. Turn and cook until brown and light, about 5 minutes.

SERVES 4 TO 6.

BLUEBERRY PANCAKES

Add ¾ cup / 175 ml fresh or frozen blueberries to the basic pancake recipe.

APPLE-CINNAMON PANCAKES

Peel and dice one large apple, preferably a somewhat tart, crispy variety, such as Gravenstein, Cortland or Granny Smith. Add to the basic pancake recipe along with ½ tsp/2 ml cinnamon.

ZESTY ORANGE PANCAKES

Zest, or grate, the rind of half an orange and add along with ¼ cup / 50 ml orange juice to the basic pancake recipe.

EXTRA-SPECIAL PANCAKES

Because we serve breakfast at our inn, we make a lot of pancakes. Regular buttermilk pancakes are popular, but from time to time we like a change in our routine. Our guests are often with us for several days or weeks, and we vary their breakfasts using the following additions.

W & R

25
BOUNTIFUL
BEGINNINGS

TIP: *Have the dry pancake ingredients made up the night before, or days in advance, and in large quantities. When you want pancakes, instead of reaching for the box, scoop out the desired quantity, add the liquids and there you are – hot, home-made pancakes!*

Baked Apple Pancakes

Certainly not traditional pancakes, these baked apple pancakes are something simple for that special Sunday brunch. Prepare all the ingredients in advance, including the sautéed apples; cooking apples such as Cortland, Granny Smith, Macintosh or Gravenstein work best. After your guests have arrived, reheat the pan and add the liquids so you will be assured the best presentation and flavour. Be prepared for oohs and ahhs.

W&R

6	COOKING APPLES	6	
2 TBSP	BUTTER OR MARGARINE	30 ML	
½ CUP	SUGAR	125 ML	
1 TBSP	AMARETTO OR	15 ML	
⅛ TSP	ALMOND EXTRACT	.5 ML	
¼ CUP	WATER	50 ML	
3	LARGE EGGS	3	
¾ CUP	MILK	175 ML	
¾ CUP	FLOUR	175 ML	
¼ TSP	SALT	1 ML	

PREHEAT OVEN TO 425° F / 220° C.

Peel and core apples, and cut them into wedges; put aside. Melt butter over medium-high heat in a 12-inch / 30-cm frying pan with an oven-safe handle. Stir in sugar, Amaretto and water, and bring to a boil. Add apple wedges; cook about 15 minutes, stirring occasionally, until apples are golden and sugar mixture begins to caramelize.

While the apples are cooking, make batter by blending the rest of the ingredients using a food processor or blender, or beat well by hand until mixture is smooth.

When apples are golden and lightly caramelized, pour in batter. Put frying pan in oven; bake 15 minutes or until puffed and golden. Be careful removing the frying pan as the handle will be hot.

Serve immediately. You may wish to serve these pancakes with maple syrup, but it isn't necessary.

SERVES 8.

2 CUPS	CRANBERRY SAUCE	500 ML
⅓ CUP	ORANGE JUICE	75 ML
½ TSP	ORANGE RIND (ZEST), GRATED	2 ML
¼ CUP	MAPLE SYRUP	50 ML

Combine all the ingredients in a saucepan. Stir over medium heat until hot, but not boiling. Serve in heavy pitchers or spoon directly onto pancakes.

SERVES 8.

CRANBERRY-MAPLE SYRUP

Pancakes are a staple at the Inn, as they were at our homes when we were growing up. What better way to feed several hungry people first thing in the morning. And this syrup really perks up your sleepy tastebuds. It's also good over ice cream or mixed with yogurt.

W & R

BREAKFAST OR DESSERT CRÊPES

Nothing impresses guests more than these glorified pancakes. Dust your breakfast or dessert plates with icing sugar, add a sprig of mint or a fresh strawberry and serve with a flourish.

W & R

3	EGGS	3
½ CUP	MILK	125 ML
½ CUP	WATER	125 ML
3 TBSP	BUTTER OR MARGARINE, MELTED	45 ML
1 CUP	FLOUR	250 ML
1 ½ TBSP	SUGAR	25 ML
¼ TSP	SALT	1 ML

Combine eggs, milk, water and butter. Blend well using a rotary beater, whisk or blender. Add flour, sugar and salt; beat until smooth. Batter should be thin but creamy. Let batter rest in refrigerator for about 1 hour. Blend well before cooking.

Lightly oil a 6-inch / 15-cm non-stick frying pan; heat until a drop of water sizzles in the pan. Pour ¼ cup / 50 ml of batter into frying pan for each crêpe, immediately rotating the pan until a thin film covers the bottom. Cook for about a minute over medium heat until lightly browned. Run a wide spatula around edge to loosen; turn over. Continue cooking for 45 seconds until lightly browned. Place cooked crêpes on plate with layers of waxed paper between. Cover crêpes; set aside and prepare filling.

Completely cooled crêpes can be stacked, wrapped in aluminum foil and refrigerated for up to 5 days, or frozen for up to 2 months.

MAKES 8 6-INCH CRÊPES.

TIP: *It's best to lightly oil a non-stick frying pan at least once when making crêpes.*

12	CRÊPES	12	
1 CUP	COTTAGE CHEESE	250 ML	
¼ CUP	SUGAR	50 ML	
4 OZ	CREAM CHEESE, SOFTENED	125 G	
1 TSP	VANILLA EXTRACT	5 ML	
½ TSP	LEMON RIND (ZEST), GRATED	2 ML	
¼ CUP	BLUEBERRIES, FRESH OR FROZEN	50 ML	
2 TBSP	BUTTER	30 ML	
1	LARGE RED-SKINNED APPLE	1	
¼ CUP	MAPLE SYRUP	50 ML	
	SOUR CREAM		
	SPRINKLE OF CINNAMON		

PREPARE BREAKFAST CRÊPES.

Combine cottage cheese, sugar, cream cheese, vanilla and lemon zest in a large bowl. Mix well. Place 1 heaping Tbsp / 15 ml of cheese filling on the centre of a crêpe. Add a few blueberries to filling. Fold one side of crêpe over filling and then fold the other side. Holding the folded sides, fold ends toward the centre. This square-shaped packet can be easily sealed by brushing a small amount of batter on the folded ends just before placing blintz into a hot frying pan with melted butter. Place blintz seam side down in frying pan. Brown both sides before serving hot.

VARIATION: WITH APPLES

Place maple syrup in a small frying pan over medium heat. Core washed apple but do not peel. Slice apple into rings and place in heated maple syrup. Sauté in bubbling syrup, turning once.

Place blintz packet on hot plate, add two or three maple apple rings and drizzle with sour cream. Serve with a light sprinkle of cinnamon.

MAKES 12 BLINTZES. SERVES 6.

BREAKFAST BLINTZES

I first tried blintzes in Toronto when I moved there in 1986. Ethnic foods like these are a wonderful addition to any family's fare. For this version, I've added a slightly Canadian touch to a traditional cheese blintz by adding blueberries, but you may also wish to try a variation with maple syrup and glazed apple slices. Prepare this recipe for breakfast some weekend morning and surprise the one you love by serving blintzes in bed along with a glass of champagne and orange juice. Wow. Is this living or what?

R

29
BOUNTIFUL
BEGINNINGS

TIP: *You can make these blintzes less rich by using light cottage cheese and light cream cheese and by substituting yogurt for sour cream.*

Citrus French Toast

We're never happy unless we alter a recipe in some fashion to reflect our own tastes and preferences. We think it's the right thing to do. The recipe then becomes our own. Not even traditional recipes are considered hallowed ground. There are few recipes, if any, that can't be altered to reflect the cook's own culinary character. Here's our modified French toast recipe.

W&R

6	THICK SLICES FRENCH BREAD	6
3	EGGS	3
½ CUP	MILK OR 10% CREAM	125 ML
2 TBSP	SUGAR	30 ML
1 TBSP	ORANGE RIND (ZEST), GRATED	15 ML
1 TSP	LEMON RIND (ZEST), GRATED	5 ML
	PINCH OF POWDERED GINGER	
1 TBSP	BUTTER	15 ML
	ICING SUGAR TO TASTE	

At least an hour or two before serving, beat eggs well in a large bowl and continue to beat while adding milk and sugar. Add zest and ginger; mix well. Lay bread slices in a single layer in a glass baking pan. Pour egg mixture over slices and let them soak for up to two hours or overnight.

Melt butter in a large heated frying pan or griddle over a medium-high heat, taking care not to burn it. Using a spatula, carefully lift bread slices into pan. Fry for 5 minutes, or until golden brown, on each side, adding more butter if necessary. Cut each slice in half. Sprinkle with icing sugar. Serve with warmed maple syrup, apple sauce or homemade jam.

SERVES 4.

Baked French Toast

4	SLICES FRENCH BREAD	4
1 TO 2	APPLES	1 TO 2
1 TBSP	LEMON JUICE	15 ML
6	EGGS, BEATEN	6
½ CUP	BUTTERMILK OR 2% MILK	125 ML
1 TSP	CINNAMON	5 ML
½ TSP	SALT	2 ML
1 TBSP	SUGAR	15 ML

PREHEAT OVEN TO 375° F / 180° C.

At least 2 hours before cooking, or as early as the night before, lay slices of French bread in an 8 ½ x 11-inch / 2-litre glass baking dish. Peel, core and slice apples into thin rings, 2 rings per slice of bread. Place apple rings in a small dish and pour lemon juice over them to keep from turning brown. In a large bowl or blender, beat together eggs, buttermilk, cinnamon and salt.

Pour almost all of the beaten egg mixture over the bread slices, reserving about ½ cup / 125 ml. Let bread rest for a couple of minutes, then turn slices over. Place 2 apple slices, slightly overlapped to form a figure eight shape, on top of each piece of French bread. Pour remaining egg mixture over apple slices. Cover baking dish with plastic wrap and refrigerate for 2 hours or overnight.

Lightly oil a baking sheet with a non-stick spray and add a few drops of vegetable oil. Lightly sprinkle sugar over bread slices. Using a spatula, carefully lift them onto baking sheet. Bake for 20 to 25 minutes, until golden brown and puffy. Serve hot with butter and your favourite fruit syrup.

SERVES 4.

This is a nice variation on an old stand-by. It's baked instead of fried, it can be made with buttermilk for a really interesting flavour, and we add apples. Once it's baked, you can simply serve and eat. Of course, if you're like us, you'll probably add syrup and bacon or sausage. But there's no need; your family will enjoy it as is.

W&R

31
BOUNTIFUL
BEGINNINGS

Breakfast on a Bagel

Bagels are becoming a popular breakfast treat. One of our fastfood coffee chains recently included them on their menu. Bagels usually contain no fat, and they are so chewy that one is all you need to feel really full. We like this recipe because it's an entire nutritious breakfast on a bun, and because it's so tasty.

W & R

¼ CUP	BUTTER OR MARGARINE	50 ML
¼ CUP	BROWN SUGAR	50 ML
½ TSP	CINNAMON	2 ML
1 TBSP	WATER	15 ML
2	BAGELS, CUT IN HALF	2
1	APPLE, CORED, CUT INTO 4 RINGS	1
4 OZ	HAM, THINLY SLICED	125 G
8	STRIPS OLD CHEDDAR CHEESE, 1 INCH/ 2.5 CM WIDE	8

Melt butter in a frying pan. Stir in brown sugar, cinnamon and water. Cook slowly over medium heat, stirring until mixture comes to a boil. Continue stirring for 1 minute. Remove from heat. Dip cut side of bagel slices in mixture and place cut side up on cookie sheet; set aside. Add apple rings to remaining brown sugar mixture. Cook over medium heat for 2 to 5 minutes, turning once or twice. Slices should be tender but crisp.

Heat broiler. Broil bagel halves 5 to 7 inches / 12 to 18 cm from heat until lightly toasted, about 1 minute. Top with 1 apple ring and 2 slices of ham; return to broiler. Broil until heated through, 1 to 2 minutes. Top with cheese strips; broil until cheese melts, about 1 minute.

SERVES 4.

BREAKFAST GRANOLA

2 CUPS	ROLLED OATS	500 ML
¼ CUP	SESAME SEEDS	50 ML
½ CUP	SUNFLOWER SEEDS	125 ML
¼ CUP	BRAN	50 ML
½ CUP	ALMONDS	125 ML
½ CUP	WHEAT GERM	125 ML
¼ CUP	PINE NUTS	50 ML
½ CUP	UNSWEETENED COCONUT	125 ML
¼ CUP	HONEY	50 ML
¼ CUP	BROWN SUGAR	50 ML
¼ CUP	VEGETABLE OIL	50 ML
½ TSP	VANILLA EXTRACT	2 ML
½ CUP	RAISINS	125 ML

Once you've made and eaten your own granola, you'll never be satisfied with the "boxed" variety again. You can leave out the things you and your family don't enjoy, adding only the ingredients you like. You can alter the fat content by cutting back on wheat germ, nuts and oil. Serve with plain yogurt or milk and you'll feel good all day.

W&R

PREHEAT OVEN TO 325° F / 160° C.

Mix oats, sesame seeds, sunflower seeds, bran, almonds, wheat germ, pine nuts and coconut in a large bowl. Heat honey, brown sugar, oil and vanilla extract in a small saucepan until mixture has liquified, taking care not to boil it. Pour this mixture over dry ingredients, stirring to coat evenly. Spread in a greased shallow baking dish and bake for 15 to 20 minutes, stirring every 5 minutes until golden brown. Mix in raisins. Store in an airtight glass container in refrigerator until ready to use. Granola freezes well, so make a double batch and freeze half of it. Add milk and fresh fruit just before eating, or serve with yogurt.

MAKES 6 CUPS.

Granola Flakes & Fruit

Not everyone likes crunchy granola. This one is made entirely out of flakes with the easier to chew sunflower seeds and our favourite, sesame seeds. We add dried apples, but you can substitute chopped dates or raisins or your favourite mixture of dried fruits.

W&R

5 CUPS	OAT FLAKES	1.25 L
1 CUP	SUNFLOWER SEEDS, HULLED AND CHOPPED	250 ML
½ CUP	SESAME SEEDS	125 ML
½ CUP	VEGETABLE OIL (OR LESS)	125 ML
½ CUP	HONEY	125 ML
5 CUPS	WHEAT FLAKES	1.25 L
2 CUPS	DRIED APPLES, CHOPPED	500 ML

PREHEAT OVEN TO 375° F / 190° C.

Mix oat flakes, seeds, oil and honey in a large bowl. Spread on a large baking sheet and toast for 3 to 5 minutes until a light golden brown. Stir often and watch carefully as the flakes will brown quickly. Remove from oven. Mix wheat flakes and apples in a large bowl. Add nut mixture and mix thoroughly. Cool. Store in sealed containers in a cool place.

MAKES ABOUT 14 CUPS / 3.5 LITRES. SERVES 24.

Nutty Maple Oats

2 CUPS	ROLLED OATS	500 ML
1 CUP	ALMONDS, COARSELY CHOPPED	250 ML
⅓ CUP	VEGETABLE OIL	75 ML
¼ CUP	MAPLE SYRUP	60 ML
½ TSP	VANILLA EXTRACT	2 ML
¼ TSP	SALT (OPTIONAL)	1 ML

PREHEAT OVEN TO 325° F / 160° C.

Mix all ingredients in a bowl. Spread on a baking sheet and toast 20 to 25 minutes until a light golden colour. Cool, break up and store in a sealed container in a cool place.

MAKES 3 CUPS / 750 ML. SERVES 6.

This home-made cereal will give the boxed varieties a run for their money. Substitute honey if you don't have maple syrup. We make it the night before when we're setting our breakfast tables, and it's nice and fresh for our guests in the morning.

W & R

35
BOUNTIFUL BEGINNINGS

Baked Fruit Compote

Compote is traditionally a chilled dish of fresh or dried fruit that has been slowly cooked in a sugar syrup. We serve our compote warm and use marmalade and orange juice instead of sugar and liqueur. It's wonderful as a side dish with pancakes or served with hot biscuits.

W & R

1 LB	DRIED MIXED FRUIT — APRICOTS, APPLES, PRUNES, ETC.	500 G
½ CUP	ORANGE MARMALADE	250 ML
½ CUP	ORANGE JUICE	250 ML
½ CUP	WATER	250 ML

Place fruit in a 9-inch / 22-cm baking pan. Stir the remaining ingredients in a small bowl. Pour over fruit, stirring gently to mix. Cover; refrigerate, stirring occasionally, for 8 hours or overnight.

Preheat oven to 350° F / 180° C. Uncover pan; bake 30 to 45 minutes or until syrup is bubbly and slightly thickened. Serve warm or cold.

SERVES 8.

2	LARGE ORANGES	2
1 CUP	PINEAPPLE CHUNKS, FRESH OR CANNED	250 ML
2 TBSP	BROWN SUGAR, FIRMLY PACKED	30 ML
1 TBSP	HONEY	15 ML
2 TBSP	FLAKED COCONUT (OPTIONAL)	30 ML
4	MARASCHINO CHERRIES OR FRESH STRAWBERRIES	4

BAKED FRUIT IN A CUP

Once you've removed the pulp, an orange becomes a cup which can be used to serve this simple, yet delicious, warm fruit dish often referred to as ambrosia. We generally wait until the large, juicy Florida oranges are available in mid-winter; if the sweet Golden Ripe pineapples are also available, you will be able to cut back on the sugar in this recipe.

W & R

PREHEAT OVEN TO 350° F / 180° C.

Cut oranges in half. Using a small serrated knife, remove fruit sections. Toss together orange sections, pineapple, brown sugar and honey in a bowl. Spoon into orange cups. Place orange cups in an 8-inch / 2-litre square baking pan. Bake 15 minutes. Sprinkle with coconut and continue baking 5 to 10 minutes until fruit is heated and coconut is lightly browned. Remove from oven and top with maraschino cherry or fresh strawberry.

SERVES 4.

37
BOUNTIFUL
BEGINNINGS

Fresh Fruit in Phyllo Bowls

An elegant way to serve fresh fruit for breakfast, brunch or as a dessert. If you want it to be more decadent, simply whip cream and add your favourite liqueur. Stir some of the fresh fruit into the cream mixture and spoon into the phyllo, then top with remaining fruit.

W & R

TIP: *Phyllo baskets are great for serving scrambled eggs sprinkled with crumbled bacon and freshly chopped parsley; or add a scoop of ice cream or yogurt before topping with fresh fruit. Just eliminate the sugar for non-dessert dishes.*

8	SHEETS FROZEN PHYLLO DOUGH, THAWED	8
¼ CUP	BUTTER OR MARGARINE, MELTED	50 ML
	POWDERED ICING SUGAR	
1 ½ CUPS	FRESH FRUIT — STRAWBERRIES, RASPBERRIES, BLUEBERRIES, KIWI, PINEAPPLE, BANANAS, ORANGES AND/OR PEACHES	375 ML
	ICING SUGAR FOR GARNISHING	

PREHEAT OVEN TO 400° F / 200° C.

Make individual bowls using any shallow dish. (We use 5-inch / 12-cm round ramekins.) Lightly oil or spray 4 ramekins with cooking spray.

After carefully removing phyllo from box, spread open sheets and cut them into quarters. Lay one quarter over dish, gently gathering to form ruffled and uneven rim. Fit into dish, allowing ends to hang over. Brush phyllo with melted butter; sprinkle with powdered sugar.

Fit second quarter of pastry over first. Brush with butter and sprinkle with sugar. Repeat layering with 5 or 6 sheets, buttering and sugaring, alternating position of sheets, until edges are well covered. Repeat for other ramekins. Bake for 4 to 6 minutes, until golden brown. Let stand 5 minutes; remove phyllo bowls from ramekins. Place each bowl in centre of large, round plate. Sprinkle icing sugar over crust. Just before serving, add prepared fresh fruit, sprinkle with sugar and serve.

SERVES 4.

From the Kitchen Stove

Breads, Pickles and Condiments

8	SLICES FRENCH BREAD	8
¼ CUP	BUTTER	50 ML
1	CLOVE GARLIC, CHOPPED	1
2 TSP	DRIED MARJORAM	10 ML
1 TBSP	FRESH PARSLEY, CHOPPED	15 ML
1 TSP	DIJON MUSTARD	5 ML
2 TBSP	PARMESAN CHEESE, GRATED	30 ML
¼ CUP	MOZZARELLA AND CHEDDAR CHEESE, GRATED AND MIXED	50 ML

CHEESE & HERB BREAD

Here's a quick and easy toasted bread recipe that's great with soup, chili or a salad. We serve it often in the cool weather. It's a great alternative to the regular garlic bread we've all come to know and love over the years. Use thick slices of lightly toasted French bread or thinner slices of untoasted rye bread.

W & R

PREHEAT BROILER.

Lightly toast French bread. Mix butter, garlic, marjoram, parsley and Dijon mustard in a small bowl. When well blended, spread the mixture on one side of the bread slices and arrange, buttered side up, on a large baking sheet. Sprinkle herbed slices with mix of mozzarella, Cheddar and Parmesan cheese. Place about 4 inches / 10 cm under the broiler and broil until brown and bubbling. Watch this process like a hawk; the bread can burn quickly.

Cut slices in half and serve hot in a basket lined with a cloth napkin.

SERVES 6 TO 8.

Pepper Cornbread

Whenever I think of cornbread, I always think of johnnycake with butter and maple syrup. That bread, made with cornmeal, was originally baked to be taken on a journey as it kept well and stood up to the rigours of rough travel. The term journey cake apparently became johnnycake over the years as the recipe was passed on by word-of-mouth. This pepper cornbread makes a wonderful accompaniment to jambalaya or beans and chili.

W

1 ½ CUPS	CORNMEAL	375 ML
½ CUP	FLOUR	125 ML
2 TSP	BAKING POWDER	10 ML
½ TSP	BAKING SODA	2 ML
½ TSP	SALT	2 ML
1 CUP	CHEDDAR CHEESE, DICED	250 ML
1 ½ CUPS	BUTTERMILK OR SOUR MILK	375 ML
¼ CUP	VEGETABLE OIL	50 ML
2	EGGS, BEATEN	2
¼ CUP	ONION, CHOPPED	50 ML
¼ CUP	RED PEPPER, DICED	50 ML
2	JALAPENO PEPPERS, DICED	2
1 OR 2	SLICES BACON	1 OR 2

PREHEAT OVEN TO 400° F / 200° C.

Mix cornmeal, flour, baking powder, baking soda, salt and cheese together in a bowl. Stir in buttermilk, oil, beaten eggs, onion and peppers, until well mixed. Batter will be fairly liquid in texture. Fry bacon in a cast iron frying pan over medium heat. When crispy, break bacon into cornmeal batter, mix and pour into still hot frying pan. Place in oven until cornbread is well browned and cooked through, about 25 to 30 minutes. Serve hot with butter.

SERVES 8.

1 CUP	SUGAR	250 ML
2 CUPS	FLOUR	500 ML
1 ½ TSP	BAKING POWDER	7 ML
½ TSP	BAKING SODA	2 ML
1 TSP	SALT	5 ML
¼ CUP	BUTTER OR MARGARINE	50 ML
1	EGG, BEATEN	1
¾ CUP	ORANGE JUICE	175 ML
1 TSP	ORANGE RIND (ZEST), GRATED	5 ML
1 CUP	CRANBERRIES	250 ML
½ CUP	SULTANA RAISINS OR CRANBERRIES	125 ML

CRANBERRY-ORANGE BREAD

We're so fortunate in the Maritimes to have such an abundant crop of fresh, wild fruits and vegetables. Just minutes from our summer home on the Kingston Peninsula there is a bog where we can fill bags and buckets with the scarlet, versatile cranberry by simply going for a walk on a sunny fall day. This recipe for cranberry orange bread has the double benefit of vitamin C from both oranges and cranberries.

W&R

PREHEAT OVEN TO 350° F / 180° C.

Mix the dry ingredients in a large bowl. Cut in butter using a pastry blender or two knives until mixture is crumbly and the crumbs about the size of peas. Blend beaten egg, juice and zest in a separate bowl. Pour into dry ingredients and stir until evenly moist. Fold in cranberries and / or raisins until just mixed. Pour into a well-greased 9 x 5-inch / 2-litre loaf pan. Bake 1 hour and 10 minutes or until bread springs back when lightly touched and a toothpick or broom straw comes out clean when inserted into centre of bread. Cool on rack for 10 minutes before removing from pan. When completely cooled, wrap well and store in a cool, dry place. This bread will keep for several weeks in the refrigerator and also freezes well. Slice and serve as is or lightly buttered at breakfast or tea time.

MAKES 1 LOAF.

Pumpkin Bread

What to do with that leftover pumpkin? Sometimes a pumpkin will sit in a corner of our kitchen until May, neither of us wanting to be the first to decide whether to toss it in the compost or cut into it, thereby becoming responsible for cooking and storing its contents. One time after Halloween, around New Year's actually, we did manage to give our "orange orphan" to a nice home, but almost every year we're stuck with it. We've now come up with some great recipes for this member of the squash family.

W&R

1 ½ CUPS	SUGAR	375 ML
2	EGGS	2
½ CUP	VEGETABLE OIL	125 ML
1 CUP	PUMPKIN PURÉE, FRESH OR CANNED	250 ML
1 ⅔ CUPS	FLOUR	400 ML
1 TSP	BAKING SODA	5 ML
¼ TSP	BAKING POWDER	1 ML
¼ TSP	SALT	1 ML
½ TSP	CLOVES	2 ML
1 TSP	CINNAMON	5 ML
½ TSP	NUTMEG	2 ML
½ TSP	ALLSPICE	2 ML
½ TSP	GINGER	2 ML

PREHEAT OVEN TO 350° F / 180° C.

Mix sugar and eggs in a large bowl; add oil and beat until smooth. Stir in pumpkin. Combine dry ingredients in a separate bowl and slowly add to egg mixture while continuing to stir. Pour into a greased 6-cup / 1.5-litre loaf pan; bake for 1 hour or until tester comes out clean and loaf springs back when you gently press on top.

Remove from loaf pan and cool on rack. Slice, butter and enjoy. Great for teatime, lunchboxes or breakfast.

MAKES 1 LOAF.

½ CUP	BUTTER	125 ML
¾ CUP	SUGAR	175 ML
2	EGGS	2
2 TBSP	ORANGE JUICE CONCENTRATE	30 ML
1	ORANGE RIND (ZEST), GRATED	1
1 ½ CUPS	FLOUR	375 ML
½ TSP	BAKING POWDER	2 ML
¼ TSP	BAKING SODA	1 ML
2 TBSP	CANDIED GINGER, DICED	30 ML
1 CUP	NUTS, CHOPPED (OPTIONAL)	250 ML

ORANGE-GINGER LOAF

Sweet loaves are a versatile food we like to have in our cupboard or freezer at the Inn. If guests arrive unexpectedly, we can put the kettle on and slice and butter our loaf to serve with tea. If we're busy and don't have time to make fresh muffins for breakfast, the loaf doubles as a starter before our cooked course. We make sweet loaves when we have a spare moment and reap the rewards when we're busy.

W & R

PREHEAT OVEN TO 350° F / 180° C.

Cream together butter and sugar in a large bowl until light and fluffy. Add eggs, orange juice and grated orange rind, beating well after each addition. Combine flour, baking powder and baking soda in a separate bowl. Stir into butter mixture. Add ginger and nuts and stir until mixture is well blended.

Pour into a well-greased 6-cup / 1.5-litre loaf pan. Bake for 1 hour or until golden brown and a toothpick inserted into the centre comes out clean.

Cool on rack before removing from pan. Bread should be completely cool before slicing. In fact, it slices best after cooling for a full 24 hours.

MAKES 1 LOAF.

Herb & Cheese Biscuits

Buttermilk is a key ingredient in light and delicious biscuits. When many of us had our own dairy cattle, buttermilk was a common ingredient and readily available. Today, this thick, slightly clotted milk is making a comeback. The addition of cayenne pepper, marjoram and thyme to these biscuits will give a bite and flavour you'll love.

W&R

2 ¼ CUPS	ALL-PURPOSE FLOUR	550 ML
2 ½ TSP	BAKING POWDER	12 ML
½ TSP	BAKING SODA	2 ML
½ TSP	SALT	2 ML
¼ TSP	MARJORAM	1 ML
¼ TSP	THYME	1 ML
¼ TSP	CAYENNE PEPPER	1 ML
½ CUP	COLD BUTTER, CUBED	125 ML
1 CUP	OLD CHEDDAR CHEESE, GRATED	250 ML
1 CUP	BUTTERMILK OR SOUR MILK	250 ML
1	EGG, LIGHTLY BEATEN	1

PREHEAT OVEN TO 425° F / 220° C.

Stir together flour, baking powder, baking soda, salt, herbs and cayenne pepper in a large bowl. Using a pastry blender, or two knives in a scissors-litreike fashion, cut butter into dry ingredients until mixture resembles coarse crumbs. Stir in cheese. Add buttermilk all at once, stirring with fork to make soft, slightly sticky dough. Press dough into a ball with floured hands. On a lightly floured surface, knead gently several times until flour is absorbed. Pat out dough into a ¾-inch / 2-cm thick round. Using a 2 ½-inch / 6-cm floured cutter, cut out rounds. Place on an ungreased baking sheet. Gather up scraps, re-form dough and cut out more rounds. Brush tops of biscuits with egg. Bake for 12 to 15 minutes.

MAKES 12 TO 16 BISCUITS.

Oatmeal Scones

1 CUP	ALL-PURPOSE FLOUR	250 ML
1 CUP	OATMEAL	250 ML
1 TSP	BAKING SODA	5 ML
1 TSP	BAKING POWDER	5 ML
½ TSP	SALT	2 ML
¼ CUP	SUGAR	50 ML
¼ CUP	SHORTENING	50 ML
1	EGG, BEATEN	1
¼ CUP	BUTTERMILK OR SOUR MILK	50 ML
	EGG OR MILK WASH	

Scones are a traditional Scottish quick bread, generally served at breakfast or for afternoon tea. The name, we understand, comes from the Stone of Destiny or Scone, the place where Scottish kings were once crowned. We cut ours in the original triangular shape, but you can make them round, square or like diamonds. Count on them being quickly eaten, no matter what the shape.

W & R

PREHEAT OVEN TO 400° F / 200° C.

Mix dry ingredients in a large bowl. Cut or rub in shortening (using your fingers) until mixture is crumbly and the crumbs are the size of peas. Beat together the egg and buttermilk and add to flour mixture, blending only until moistened.

On a floured surface, pat dough down until 1½ inches / 3.5 cm thick. Cut into triangles and place on a lightly greased baking sheet; brush with egg or milk. Bake 12 to 15 minutes or until golden brown. Serve warm with butter and jam.

MAKES 12 TO 16 SCONES.

Whole Wheat Sour Cream Cinnamon Rolls

½ CUP	LUKEWARM WATER	125 ML
¼ CUP	GRANULATED SUGAR	50 ML
1 TBSP	FAST-RISING YEAST	15 ML
¼ CUP	BUTTER	50 ML
½ CUP	SOUR CREAM	125 ML
	PINCH OF SALT	
2	EGGS	2
1 ½ CUPS	WHOLE WHEAT FLOUR	375 ML
2 CUPS	ALL-PURPOSE FLOUR	500 ML

Filling

⅓ CUP	BUTTER OR MARGARINE, MELTED	75 ML
1 ½ CUPS	BROWN SUGAR	375 ML
1 TBSP	CINNAMON	15 ML
1 TSP	GINGER	5 ML
½ CUP	RAISINS	125 ML
½ CUP	PECANS, CHOPPED	125 ML
¼ CUP	MAPLE SYRUP	50 ML

When we made this recipe on our television show, we received a charming letter, written in pencil, from an eight-year-old viewer. He told us how much he liked our show and asked for a copy of our cinnamon "rool" recipe. On the flip side of his letter was a note from his dad telling us that they both enjoyed *Tide's Table*. He said they were going to make the rolls together. Some days we can't wait to pick up the mail.

W&R

PREHEAT OVEN TO 350° F / 180° C.

Add lukewarm water in a small bowl or measuring cup; dissolve 1 tsp / 5 ml of the sugar and sprinkle with yeast. Let stand for 10 minutes, until frothy, making sure that you keep it away from drafts.

Melt butter in a medium saucepan over low heat; transfer to large bowl, add remaining sugar, sour cream and salt. Beat in eggs, add yeast mixture and gradually add flour. Beat until smooth with a wooden spoon, about 2 or 3 minutes.

Gradually add more flour, beating well with a spoon to form a sticky dough. Lightly flour a flat surface and knead dough, adding any remaining flour. Knead well for about 10 minutes. Dough should be soft, smooth and elastic. Place dough in a greased bowl, turning well to grease all over. Cover with plastic wrap and let dough rise in a warm, draft-

TIP: *To provide a warm, draft-free spot for your bread, preheat oven on warm, turn it off and place the bread in the oven with the oven light on.*

free place for about 1½ hours or place the bowl in refrigerator overnight. Dough should double in bulk.

Cut dough in half. Set half aside in a bowl covered with a warm cloth and place the other half on a lightly floured surface. Roll out dough into a rectangle about ½ inch / 1 cm thick. Brush with melted butter. In a small bowl, mix brown sugar, cinnamon and ginger. Spread half this mixture over the buttered dough; sprinkle with half the raisins and half the pecans.

From the long side of the rectangle, roll up dough like a jelly roll. Pinch ends to seal. Cut roll into 1-inch / 2.5-cm pieces. Line an 8 ½ x 11-inch / 3-litre pan with foil and oil well. Place rolls into pan, about 4 across. Repeat with other half of dough.

Cover and let rise in a warm place for about 45 minutes. Bake for 25 to 30 minutes. Remove from oven, drizzle with maple syrup and let cool 20 minutes.

To "gild the lily," ice with a mixture of ½ cup / 125 ml icing sugar mixed with a little milk (about 2 tsp / 10 ml). Serve warm.

MAKES 16 LARGE ROLLS.

Hot Cross Buns

One of my favourite childhood memories is of Mum making hot cross buns every March. Even when I became an adult, she still made them and shared them with me. As Mum got older, I panicked, thinking the day might come when I'd no longer have homemade hot cross buns. Then one day I started making my own, and guess what? I shared them with Mum.

¼ CUP	LUKEWARM WATER	50 ML
1 TBSP	LIGHT BROWN SUGAR	15 ML
2 TBSP	YEAST	30 ML
1 ½ CUPS	SCALDED MILK	375 ML
½ CUP	BUTTER OR MARGARINE	125 ML
½ CUP	BROWN SUGAR	125 ML
1 ½ TSP	SALT	7 ML
2	EGGS, BEATEN	2
4 ⅓ CUPS	ALL-PURPOSE FLOUR, SIFTED	1 L
2 TSP	CINNAMON	10 ML
1 TSP	CLOVES	5 ML
½ TSP	NUTMEG	2 ML
½ CUP	CURRANTS	125 ML
⅓ CUP	CITRON, FINELY DICED (OR RAISINS)	75 ML

ICING

2 TBSP	HOT MILK	30 ML
	ICING SUGAR TO THICKEN	
1	LEMON RIND (ZEST), GRATED	1

PREHEAT OVEN TO 400° F / 200° C.

Add lukewarm water to a small bowl or measuring cup; dissolve 1 Tbsp / 15 ml of light brown sugar and sprinkle with yeast. Let stand for 10 minutes, until frothy. Be sure to keep it away from drafts. Scald the milk and add the butter, sugar and salt. Beat the eggs until they are light and combine with the milk mixture and the yeast. Sift 3 cups / 750 ml of the flour; combine with the spices in a mixing bowl; then add the yeast mixture. Beat for 4 minutes to form a sponge. Toss the currants and citron with ½ cup / 125 ml of the flour and mix it with the sponge. If necessary, add more flour to make a firm dough. Beat well and set the dough in a pan of warm water to rise, covered with a towel. When dough is light, push it down well and form it into 2 dozen balls. Place them in a long well-greased pan, loosely covered with a towel, to rise again. This will take about 45 minutes. Bake about 20 minutes. Remove from the oven and brush with melted butter.

Mix hot milk with powdered sugar to make a thick icing. Add grated lemon rind. Fill pastry bag and when buns are cool, form a cross on the top of each bun with the icing.

MAKES 2 DOZEN BUNS.

Bagels or Soft Pretzels

4 ½ CUPS	BREAD FLOUR	1050 ML
1 ½ CUPS	LUKEWARM WATER	375 ML
2 TBSP	SUGAR	30 ML
2 ¼ TSP	YEAST	7 ML
1 TBSP	SALT	15 ML
	SESAME SEEDS, POPPY SEEDS OR	
	CARAWAY SEEDS FOR GARNISHING	
	COARSE SALT FOR PRETZELS	

Although bagels are made with yeast and flour like most raised breads, they have a personality all their own. Bagels are boiled in water before they're baked, giving them a chewy crust. They are also made without fat and eggs which makes them popular with people on restricted diets. You can eat them just as they are, or toast and serve them with jam or marmalade. Pretzels are also becoming a popular snack because they don't contain fat. Just go easy on the salt.

W & R

PREHEAT OVEN TO 375° F / 190° C.

Sift four into a large mixing bowl and make a "well" in the centre. Pour water into the well and sprinkle sugar and yeast into water. Let sit in a warm place for 5 or 6 minutes, allowing yeast to start working. When yeast is foamy, add salt and stir the flour into the yeast mixture to form a soft dough. Turn out onto floured surface and knead for about 10 minutes. Add flour as required to stop dough from sticking. When dough is smooth and elastic in texture, place into greased bowl, cover with plastic wrap and let rise in a warm place for 12 to 15 minutes. In the meantime, heat about 2 quarts / 2 litres of water in a large Dutch oven or pan on top of stove. Bring to a boil and then reduce heat to let simmer.

Punch down dough and divide into 16 equal parts for bagels or 32 pieces for pretzels. Roll dough by hand into long sausage shapes about 8 or 9 inches long. For bagels, join each sausage piece into a circle. For pretzels, make sausage shaped strips about 12 inches long and cross ends of dough over each other and press to secure. Place on a lightly floured baking sheet, cover with waxed paper and let rise in warm place for about 20 minutes. Add bagels or pretzels to simmering water a few at a time, as space allows. Turn once while simmering for about 6 minutes. Lift out of hot water and let dry briefly on a clean cotton towel. Sprinkle bagels with poppy, sesame or caraway seeds and bake on ungreased baking sheet for about 35 minutes. Sprinkle pretzels with coarse salt and bake for about 15 minutes. Pretzels will take less time to bake. They should be lightly browned and cooked through.

MAKES 16 BAGELS OR 32 PRETZELS.

1 ½ CUPS	ALL-PURPOSE FLOUR	375 ML
1 TSP	BAKING SODA	5 ML
1 TSP	BAKING POWDER	5 ML
1 TSP	CINNAMON	5 ML
¼ TSP	NUTMEG	1 ML
¼ TSP	GROUND OR POWDERED CLOVES	1 ML
	PINCH OF SALT	
2	EGGS	2
¼ CUP	WHITE SUGAR	50 ML
¼ CUP	MAPLE SYRUP	50 ML
1 TBSP	MOLASSES	15 ML
⅔ CUP	VEGETABLE OIL	150 ML
¼ CUP	PINEAPPLE, CRUSHED AND DRAINED	50 ML
1 CUP	CARROT, GRATED	250 ML
½ CUP	RAISINS	125 ML
1	WHOLE ORANGE, FINELY CHOPPED	1
1 TSP	LEMON PEEL (ZEST), GRATED	5 ML

$100 Muffins

It's not often you can put a price tag on one of your original recipes. Our marvellous Maritime muffin recipe won a prize of $100 in an Uptown Saint John baking contest. Just minutes before the contest started, the muffins were taken out of the oven at the Inn. I cradled the hot pan on my lap as Willa drove frantically, dropping me off at the City Market, where the contest was getting underway. I rushed in with my still steaming muffins. And the rest, as they say, is history. Talk about team work.

R

53
FROM THE KITCHEN STOVE

PREHEAT OVEN TO 350° F / 180° C.

Combine flour, baking soda, baking powder, spices and salt in a large mixing bowl. Whip eggs in a smaller bowl with a hand mixer at high speed; gradually add sugar, maple syrup and molasses while beating. Continue to beat while gradually adding vegetable oil. Using a spoon, fold in pineapple, carrot, raisins, orange and lemon peel. Fold wet mixture into dry ingredients and mix by hand. Batter should be thick but moist. If it is too dry, add a small amount of orange juice. Fill well-greased muffin cups three-quarters full and bake for 20 to 25 minutes. Muffins should spring back to the touch when done.

MAKES 12 LARGE OR 16 SMALLER MUFFINS.

TIP: *You can put the whole orange into the food processor, chop it up and use the entire fruit. You may alternatively grate the rind and use the juice. If you use this method, you may also have to adjust the recipe by adding an additional 1 Tbsp / 15 ml orange juice.*

Pineapple-Double Cream Muffins

Our guests love the hot, home-made muffins we offer with breakfast, but we've encountered a number of people who can't eat nuts. These muffins keep everyone happy. We put nuts in only half the pans. It generally works out perfectly and our staff happily agree to eat any leftovers.

W & R

3 OZ	CREAM CHEESE, SOFTENED	90 G
1 CUP	SUGAR (OR LESS)	250 ML
1 TSP	VANILLA EXTRACT	5 ML
1	EGG, BEATEN	1
2 CUPS	ALL-PURPOSE FLOUR, SIFTED	500 ML
1 TSP	BAKING SODA	5 ML
1 TSP	SALT	5 ML
½ CUP	SOUR CREAM	125 ML
19-OZ CAN	PINEAPPLE, CRUSHED AND DRAINED	540-ML CAN
½ CUP	ALMONDS, SLICED OR WALNUTS, CHOPPED	125 ML

PREHEAT OVEN TO 350° F / 180° C.

Beat cream cheese, sugar and vanilla in a large bowl until smooth. Blend in egg. In a separate bowl, mix flour, baking soda and salt; add to cream cheese mixture alternately with sour cream. Fold in drained pineapple, being careful not to over mix.

Sprinkle nuts in bottom of well-oiled muffin tins and fill three-quarters full with batter. Bake for 25 to 30 minutes or until muffin springs back when lightly touched and toothpick inserted in centre comes out clean.

Cool on rack for 10 minutes before removing from tins. Serve warm.

MAKES 12 TO 14 MUFFINS.

1½ CUPS	ALL-PURPOSE FLOUR	375 ML
½ CUP	SUGAR	125 ML
2 TSP	BAKING POWDER	10 ML
¼ TSP	SALT	1 ML
1	EGG, BEATEN	1
¼ CUP	VEGETABLE OIL	50 ML
½ CUP	MILK	125 ML
2 TSP	LEMON JUICE	10 ML
1½ CUPS	RASPBERRIES, FRESH OR FROZEN	375 ML
1 TSP	LEMON RIND (ZEST), GRATED	5 ML

Streusel Topping

¼ CUP	BROWN SUGAR	50 ML
¼ CUP	FLOUR	50 ML
1 TBSP	BUTTER, MELTED	15 ML
1 TSP	LEMON RIND (ZEST), GRATED	5 ML
¼ CUP	PECANS, CHOPPED (OPTIONAL)	50 ML

We're fortunate to have an abundance of raspberries. Our guests from Ontario and the United States are always delighted to find homemade raspberry jam on the breakfast table. These muffins get everyone off to a great start. We like to freeze a few berries to surprise our winter guests with a taste of summer.

W&R

PREHEAT OVEN TO 350° F / 180° C.

Sift together dry ingredients in a large bowl. In a small bowl, beat together egg, oil, milk and lemon juice. Pour into flour mixture, stirring until dry ingredients are just moistened (the batter should be lumpy). Lightly fold in raspberries and lemon rind. Spoon into oiled muffin tins, filling three-quarters full. Combine the streusel topping ingredients in a small bowl and sprinkle on muffin dough.

Bake for 20 minutes or until muffin springs back when lightly touched and a toothpick inserted in centre comes out clean. Cool on rack for 10 minutes. Remove from muffin tins and serve.

MAKES 12 MUFFINS.

Spicy Apple Muffins

Muffins used to be so boring. Bran, oatmeal and raisins were the most exciting ingredients. Now we have muffin stores with 57 varieties. The sky's the limit when it comes to adding unusual ingredients and toppings. Do you have more pears than apples? No problem, use pears. Have fun with your muffin recipes; maybe you'll invent a new one.

W&R

2	COOKING APPLES	2
2 CUPS	ALL-PURPOSE FLOUR	500 ML
½ CUP	BROWN SUGAR, PACKED	125 ML
2 TSP	BAKING POWDER	10 ML
1 TSP	BAKING SODA	5 ML
½ TSP	SALT	2 ML
1 CUP	BUTTERMILK	250 ML
¼ CUP	VEGETABLE OIL	50 ML
1 TSP	VANILLA EXTRACT	5 ML
1	EGG, LIGHTLY BEATEN	1
½ CUP	CHOPPED WALNUTS (OPTIONAL)	125 ML

Topping

2 TBSP	BROWN SUGAR	30 ML
¼ TSP	CINNAMON	1 ML
¼ TSP	NUTMEG	1 ML

PREHEAT OVEN TO 400° F / 200° C.

Peel, core and dice apples; set aside. Mix flour, sugar, baking powder, soda and salt in a large bowl. Beat buttermilk, oil, vanilla and egg in a small bowl until blended; stir into flour mixture until flour is moistened (the batter should be lumpy). Fold in apples and walnuts, if desired.

Mix sugar and spices in a small bowl for topping. Spoon batter into muffin tins that have been oiled or lined with paper baking cups; sprinkle with topping mixture. Bake 20 to 25 minutes or until a toothpick inserted in the centre of a muffin comes out clean. Cool 5 minutes on a wire rack before removing from pan; serve warm, or cool on wire rack and reheat in microwave oven (10 seconds per muffin).

MAKES 1 DOZEN MUFFINS.

PICKLED MUSHROOMS

½ CUP	ONION, CHOPPED	125 ML
1	CLOVE GARLIC, CHOPPED FINELY	1
¼ CUP	PARSLEY, CHOPPED	50 ML
2	BAY LEAVES	2
⅛ TSP	PEPPER	.5 ML
½ TSP	THYME LEAVES, DRIED	2 ML
2 CUPS	DRY WHITE WINE	500 ML
½ CUP	OLIVE OR VEGETABLE OIL	125 ML
2 TBSP	LEMON JUICE	30 ML
1 LB	FRESH SMALL MUSHROOMS	450 G

Combine all ingredients except mushrooms in a large saucepan and mix well. Add mushrooms. (If you are unable to find small, bite-size mushrooms, slice larger ones, leaving the stems attached.) Bring to a boil, then reduce heat, and simmer for 8 to 10 minutes or until mushrooms are tender. Let mushrooms cool. Refrigerate in a large covered glass bowl or jar at least 1 hour, or until ready to use. Mushrooms will keep refrigerated for 1 week. Serve as an hors d'oeuvre or on lettuce leaves as an appetizer.

MAKES 4 TO 6 CUPS / 1.5 TO 2 LITRES.

It dates us, but we can remember when refrigeration was a luxury and freezing only occurred in the depths of winter. Back then, vegetables as delicate and seasonal as mushrooms were either canned or pickled for use later in the year. Canned or preserved mushrooms were okay in soups and stews, but pickled mushrooms were always considered a delicacy. Now fresh mushrooms are readily available throughout the year. However, we still love the slightly decadent feeling of opening a jar of our own pickled mushrooms.

W&R

TIP: *Never wash mushrooms to clean them. Simply wipe them with a damp cloth or small brush. Their real flavour is in the skin, so don't peel them. Also, try not to remove the stems; they help keep mushrooms from shrinking during cooking. Store in an open glass jar or paper bag, not in a plastic bag or sealed container, or these delicate vegetables will sweat and quickly deteriorate.*

Spicy Pickled Pears

1 ½ CUPS	SUGAR	375 ML
⅔ CUP	WHITE WINE VINEGAR	150 ML
1	STICK CINNAMON	1
6	CLOVES	6
2 LBS	PEARS	1 KG

When we lived in Toronto, we had a lovely backyard. We planted a vegetable garden and had a rhubarb patch and a pear tree. Every other fall we would have more pears than we could possibly consume, so we began pickling them. Spicy pickled pears are especially good with pork or lamb, and since pears are readily available all year round now. So you can make this recipe anytime.

W & R

Combine sugar, vinegar and spices in a saucepan. Bring to a boil over medium heat, stirring until sugar has dissolved.

Peel, halve and core pears. Add to the syrup and bring to a boil. Reduce heat, cover and poach very gently for about 45 minutes, turning pears a few times during cooking.

Place pear halves in hot sterilized jars. Fill with boiling syrup, discarding spices; add lids. Store in a cool, dry place.

MAKES 6 8-OZ / 250-ML JARS.

4 LBS	SMALL YOUNG BEETS	2 KG
3 CUPS	WHITE OR CIDER VINEGAR	750 ML
1 CUP	WATER	250 ML
1 TBSP	SALT	15 ML
1 TSP	GROUND ALLSPICE	5 ML
2 TBSP	WHOLE CLOVES, TIED IN A CHEESE-CLOTH BAG	30 ML

Scrub beets thoroughly, leaving root and 1-inch / 2.5-cm stem. Cook in lightly salted water until tender, about 25 minutes. Dip in cold water and remove skins by cutting off the root and stem with a sharp knife and sliding the skin off with your fingers.

Combine the rest of the ingredients in a saucepan and boil for 5 minutes. Remove spice bag and keep syrup hot until needed.

Pack beets into hot, sterilized jars and completely cover them with the hot syrup, leaving about ⅛ inch / 3 mm of headspace. Seal immediately, label and store in a cool, dry place.

MAKES ABOUT 6 TO 8 8-OZ / 250-ML JARS.

PICKLED BABY BEETS

Making pickled beets is an act of love. It's time-consuming, fussy, messy work and you end up with hands dyed red. But it's worth it. Pickled beets go with most lunch or supper dishes. They are a must on the Christmas dinner table, and they're great with a meat sandwich or meat loaf. My mother-in-litreaw gives me pickled beets, so I know she loves me.

W

TIP: *When preparing beets for cooking, leave the fine root tip and about one inch of stem attached or they will bleed out most of their brilliant red colour, leaving you with a pale, colourless vegetable.*

MUSTARD PICKLES

Involve the whole family in making this condiment and you'll find the preparation time is reduced. Besides, it's good fun and a chance to do some talking. By the way, chopped onion may be substituted for the silverskin onions. As our son discovered, it can take forever to peel the small silverskin variety.

W & R

20	LARGE CUCUMBERS	20
2 LBS	SILVERSKIN ONIONS, PEELED	900 G
2	HEADS CAULIFLOWER	2
2	RED PEPPERS	2
1	BUNCH CELERY	1
	WHITE PICKLING VINEGAR	
10 CUPS	SUGAR	2.5 L
2 TBSP	CELERY SEED	30 ML
4 TBSP	MUSTARD SEED	60 ML
4 CUPS	SUGAR	1 L
4 TBSP	DRY MUSTARD	60 ML
3 TBSP	TURMERIC	45 ML
2 CUPS	FLOUR	500 ML
	ENOUGH WHITE VINEGAR TO FORM A PASTE	

Peel cucumbers. Seed them by cutting them in half lengthwise and using a spoon to scoop out the seeds. Cut cucumbers into ½-inch / 1-cm pieces and place in a large, deep, non-aluminum pot or pottery crock. Cut all other vegetables in a similar manner and add them to the pot. Add 1 cup / 250 ml pickling salt and 1 cup / 250 ml water, and let sit for at least 12 hours or overnight.

The next day, drain the vegetables and place them in a large stainless steel pot with a heavy bottom. (The pickles are more likely to burn on the bottom of a lightweight pot.) Add vinegar to a depth of about 3 inches / 7 cm below the top of vegetables. Add the sugar, celery and mustard seed. Mix the sugar, dry mustard, flour, turmeric and white vinegar to make a paste. Add the paste to the vegetables and mix well. Cook uncovered over low to medium heat, for about 3 hours. When done, pickles thicken and sauce becomes a deep clear yellow. Bottle in sterilized bottles and enjoy. Mustard pickles may be eaten immediately. They'll also last 2 to 3 years if stored in a cool, dark place or in a refrigerator.

MAKES ABOUT 16 8-OZ / 250-ML JARS.

CHOW CHOW

4 TO 5 LBS	GREEN TOMATOES	2 KG
3 LBS	ONIONS	1.5 KG
1 TBSP	PICKLING SALT	15 ML
2	RED PEPPERS	2
¼ CUP	MIXED PICKLING SPICE (IN A CHEESECLOTH BAG)	50 ML
	WHITE VINEGAR	
	SUGAR TO TASTE	

Chow chow is as individual as the person who makes it. Although this is Willa's mother's recipe, we never cook our tomatoes quite as long as she did so our "chow" looks more colourful than hers. We often prepare chow chow while standing outside on a fine September day. Who can resist those last warm days of summer? The breeze makes cutting the onions a less tearful job. Chow chow is Willa's favourite pickle. She's been known to pack it when we travel. It even inspired Vicki Gabereau on CBC Radio to dub Willa the "Queen of Condiments."

R

Chop tomatoes and onions and sprinkle with pickling salt. Let sit overnight. The next day, drain off the juice. Add two diced red peppers. Bury cheesecloth bag of mixed pickling spice deep into the pot.

Cover three-quarters of the pickle mixture with white vinegar. Cook over medium heat, stirring often until pickle is soft. Add sugar to taste (the pickles should have a nice sweet and sour flavour). Pack into hot sterilized jars; cover with hot liquid and seal. Wait at least a month before serving.

MAKES 8 TO 10 8-OZ / 250-ML JARS.

Cucumber-Celery Relish

As a young bride and mother, I was fortunate to move next door to the Hutt family in Nova Scotia. We called them Nanny and Granddad and felt very much a part of their family. Mr. Hutt shared his homemade rolls with us, and Mrs. Hutt shared her vegetable garden. After providing the cucumbers, she also gave me her recipe for relish. I hope you'll try it, and, in keeping with the spirit in which it was given to me, please share it with someone else.

W

6	CUCUMBERS, DICED	6
2 CUPS	CELERY, DICED	500 ML
3	ONIONS, CHOPPED	3
3	GREEN PEPPERS, CHOPPED	3
1	RED PEPPER, CHOPPED	1
3 CUPS	WHITE VINEGAR	750 ML
3 Tbsp	FLOUR	45 ML
1½ CUPS	WHITE SUGAR	375 ML
⅔ TSP	TURMERIC	3 ML
	SALT TO TASTE	

Combine vegetables in a large saucepan; cover with 1 quart / 1 litre water and sprinkle with 1 Tbsp / 15 ml salt. Let stand overnight. Drain off the juice. Combine vinegar, flour, sugar, turmeric and salt in a small saucepan. Cook over medium heat until blended. Remove from heat and stir into vegetables.

Return large saucepan to medium heat and bring to a boil, stirring occasionally. Reduce heat and simmer, stirring frequently for approximately 15 minutes or until liquid has thickened but still covers vegetables.

Pour relish into hot sterilized jars, leaving ¼ inch / 5 mm of headspace. Store in a cool, dark, dry place.

MAKES 12 8-OZ / 250-ML JARS.

TIP: *Pickles, like fine wines, improve with age. Although it's hard to resist eating them immediately, they will be tastier in a week or two.*

Apple & Green Tomato Chutney

2 CUPS	GREEN APPLES, PEELED AND CHOPPED	500 ML
3 CUPS	GREEN TOMATOES, CHOPPED	750 ML
1½ CUPS	RAISINS	375 ML
1 CUP	ONION, MINCED	250 ML
1	CLOVE GARLIC, CHOPPED	1
1½ TSP	SALT	7 ML
1 TBSP	LEMON JUICE	15 ML
1 TBSP	LEMON PEEL (ZEST), GRATED	15 ML
2 CUPS	WHITE VINEGAR	500 ML
¼ TSP	CAYENNE PEPPER	1 ML
1 TBSP	ALLSPICE	15 ML
1 TBSP	CLOVES	15 ML
2½ CUPS	BROWN SUGAR	625 ML
2 TBSP	MUSTARD SEED	30 ML
2 TBSP	GINGER ROOT, CHOPPED AND WRAPPED IN A GAUZE BAG	30 ML

Chutney comes from the Hindi word "catni," meaning any tangy condiment of fruit, sugar and spices. Chutney is great with curry, but we also eat it with roasted pork, turkey, seafood and beef. The wonderfully spicy and subtle fruitiness of this chutney is a perfect foil for the rich flavour of many meat dishes.

W & R

Place all ingredients in a large, heavy pot and bring to a boil. Reduce heat and simmer for about 2 hours or until thick. Remove ginger root. Fill and seal canning jars. Process in a boiling water bath for 10 minutes. Store in a cool, dry place.

MAKES 8 TO 10 8-OZ / 250-ML JARS.

Rhubarb & Apple Chutney

If you have rhubarb growing in your garden, you know how difficult it is to keep ahead of its proliferation when the warmth of late spring and early summer causes it to grow with a vengeance. One use for extra rhubarb is this chutney recipe. Like other chutneys, it's delicious with any meat dish or simply with bread and cheese.

W & R

8 CUPS	RHUBARB, DICED	2 L
5 CUPS	APPLES, DICED AND PEELED	1.25 L
1½ CUPS	ONION, CHOPPED	375 ML
1	CLOVE GARLIC, CRUSHED	1
5 CUPS	BROWN SUGAR	1.25 L
½ CUP	WATER	125 ML
1½ CUPS	WHITE OR CIDER VINEGAR	375 ML
1 CUP	RAISINS	250 ML
1 TSP	SALT	5 ML
1 TSP	CINNAMON	5 ML
1 TSP	WHOLE CLOVES	5 ML
2	SMALL PIECES OF GINGER ROOT	2

Combine all ingredients except cloves and ginger root in a heavy stainless steel saucepan. Tie the cloves and ginger root in a gauze bag and add to the centre of the pot, allowing for easy removal of the spices before bottling. Bring mixture to a boil over medium-high heat. Reduce heat to medium and simmer, uncovered, until thick (about 1½ hours), stirring occasionally. Pour into hot sterilized jars and seal. Process in a boiling water bath for 10 minutes.

MAKES 8 8-OZ / 250-ML JARS.

6	CLOVES GARLIC	6
¾ CUP	YELLOW MUSTARD SEEDS, FINELY GROUND	175 ML
¾ CUP	WATER	175 ML
⅓ CUP	CIDER VINEGAR	75 ML
4 TBSP	OLIVE OR VEGETABLE OIL	60 ML
1 TSP	PEPPERCORNS, COARSELY CRACKED	5 ML
1 TSP	FRESH HORSERADISH, GRATED	5 ML
1½ TSP	SALT	7 ML
2 TBSP	HONEY OR MAPLE SYRUP	30 ML

Hot Garlic Mustard

Mustard is one of those condiments that comes in many different varieties, strengths, flavours and colours. Interestingly, the mustard plant belongs to the same family as broccoli, Brussels sprouts, collard and kale. Generally, a mustard's flavour and fire are dictated by the type of mustard seed used, along with the other primary spices and liquid it's mixed with. Once you open a bottle of mustard, it should usually be refrigerated.

R

*P*lace garlic and 1 cup / 250 ml water in a small saucepan. Bring to a boil and cook at a high heat for 10 to 12 minutes, or until the garlic is very soft. Drain well. Cool garlic cloves and skin them. Place them in a blender or food processor with the remaining ingredients. Purée until fairly smooth and well mixed, frequently scraping the sides of the container. Transfer to a clean, dry jar or bowl, cover tightly and refrigerate. Like all pickles, the taste of mustard improves with age. Wait at least a week, if possible, before using.

MAKES ABOUT 1½ CUPS.

65
FROM THE
KITCHEN STOVE

RHUBARB SPREAD

Rhubarb is definitely an acquired, adult taste. I can remember Dad actually smacking his lips over a bowl of stewed rhubarb. Mum always tried to pick the first feed for Mother's Day. My parents grew enough for everyone they knew and from May to August folks arrived for their trunkload of "barb" and a cup of tea and conversation on the sun porch. Sharing rhubarb is now a family tradition, and people are always so surprised and delighted to be offered something for free. Need rhubarb? Drop by.

W

6 CUPS	RHUBARB, CHOPPED INTO SMALL CHUNKS	1.5 L
¾ CUP	WATER	175 ML
5 CUPS	SUGAR	1.25 L
2 TBSP	CANDIED GINGER	30 ML
1 TSP	CINNAMON	5 ML
1	ORANGE (ZEST), GRATED	1

Stir rhubarb, water and sugar until mixture comes to a boil in a deep pot with a heavy bottom over medium heat. Reduce heat; add ginger, cinnamon and orange zest. Simmer for about 45 minutes, stirring often so that the mixture doesn't burn. When mixture is quite thick, pour it into sterilized glass jars and seal with hot wax.

Although delicious as a spread, this can also be used like chutney.

MAKES 8 OR 9 8-OZ / 250-ML JARS.

Gooseberry Jam with Lemon Balm

4	LARGE APPLES	4
8 CUPS	GOOSEBERRIES	2 L
2 TBSP	LEMON JUICE	30 ML
1 TBSP	FRESH LEMON BALM, CHOPPED	15 ML
3 CUPS	WATER	375 ML
3 CUPS	SUGAR	375 ML
1/3 CUP	LEMON BALM LEAVES	75 ML

Roughly chop washed, stemmed, unpeeled apples and place them in a large saucepan. Wash and stem gooseberries and add to pan with lemon juice, lemon balm and water. Cover and bring to a boil; reduce heat and simmer about 30 minutes or until fruit is very soft. Add sugar and stir over medium-high heat until sugar is dissolved. Boil, uncovered and without stirring, for about 15 minutes or until thick. Let stand 5 minutes; stir in extra lemon balm.

Pour into hot, sterilized jars, and seal with wax when cold.

MAKES 6 TO 8 8-OZ / 250-ML JARS.

Gooseberries are an old-fashioned berry. Our grandmothers always had gooseberry jam in their cold room, but it's a flavour their grandchildren are often not familiar with. This is a wonderful, updated recipe, using lemon balm to produce a delicate lemon flavour. Lemon balm is a member of the mint family. Gooseberries grow on a decorative bush. Both of them grow at our Inn.

W & R

67
FROM THE
KITCHEN STOVE

Rhubarb-Strawberry Jam

Rhubarb seems to have played a significant part in many a childhood. We're amazed at the number of guests at the Inn who comment on the jam made from our own rhubarb. When it's in season, we have difficulty keeping ahead of this fast-growing vegetable. Although it is often used like a fruit, rhubarb is actually a member of the buckwheat family. Rhubarb flourishes in our garden in late spring and early summer. Here's a way to enjoy its flavour year round.

W & R

TIP: *Rhubarb should be picked frequently to insure a good yield. Cut down any flowering stalks so the plant produces new stalks and leaves. Don't trim and discard the sweet, white bottom part of the stalks. They're delicious. But rhubarb leaves contain oxalic acid and are often toxic.*

5 CUPS	RHUBARB, CUT INTO 1-INCH / 2-CM CHUNKS	1.25 L
5 CUPS	WHITE SUGAR	1.25 L
19-OZ CAN	CRUSHED PINEAPPLE, INCLUDING JUICE	540-ML CAN
2	ENVELOPES STRAWBERRY JELLY POWDER	2

Combine rhubarb, sugar, jelly powder and pineapple in a deep pan with a heavy bottom, over medium heat. Stir well until mixture comes to a full boil. Simmer for 3 minutes. Pour into sterilized bottles and seal with wax. This jam is delicious on toast.

MAKES 6 TO 8 8-OZ / 250-ML JARS.

20 CUPS	CRAB APPLES	5 L
8 CUPS	WATER	2 L
8 CUPS	GRANULATED SUGAR	2 L

*P*repare apples by washing them, cutting them in half and removing stems. Combine apples and water in a large saucepan or stock pot. Bring to a boil; reduce heat and simmer, uncovered, for about 30 minutes, until apples are soft and mushy. Crush the hot cooked fruit with a potato masher, taking care not to burn your hand or arm. Transfer the fruit to a colander lined with a double layer of cheesecloth or a proper jelly bag. Hang the bag from a hook or cupboard handle over a bowl and let juice drain overnight.

The next morning, measure the juice. There should be about 8 cups / 2 litres. Dispose of the apple pulp in your compost pile.

PECTIN TEST:

Boil juice, uncovered, in a heavy saucepan for 3 minutes. Remove from heat and measure 1 tsp / 5 ml of juice into 1 Tbsp / 15 ml of rubbing alcohol in a small dish. Blend and let stand 30 seconds. If a jelly-like mass forms at the bottom of the dish, the juice contains sufficient pectin and requires no further boiling. If a heavy clot does not form, continue boiling, testing frequently until the jelly mass forms. Discard alcohol mixture.

Once jelly mass forms, measure sugar, allowing 1 cup / 250 ml per cup of juice. If a longer boiling has been required, allow ¾ cup / 175 ml sugar per cup of juice. Slowly add sugar to the hot juice, stirring until well blended. Quickly bring to a boil, skimming off foam with a spoon or ladle as it forms. Boil from 3 to 10 minutes or until the mixture gels.

JELLY TEST:

Dip a large metal spoon into the liquid and hold it, once filled, well above the preserving kettle. Tilt spoon until syrup runs over the side. When jelly stage is reached, the liquid will stop flowing in a stream and divide into two distinct drops that run together and leave spoon in a "sheet." Jelly sets at 218° F / 103° C to 220° F / 104° C on a candy thermometer.

Remove immediately from heat. Let stand 1 minute while removing foam with a cold, clean spoon.

If you or your neighbours have a flowering crab-apple tree, then get ready to make jelly. These small red gems are full of a natural pectin, colour and flavour that we've not found in any other apples. Some trees don't produce fruit large enough for good jelly, so try and find crab-apples the size of walnuts or larger. Pick the fruit early in the season before it over-ripens. If you can't acquire the flowering kind, then regular crab-apples will work nicely.

W & R

TIP: *Add 2 or 3 whole cloves to the jar before pouring in the hot jelly. This will give the jelly a wonderful spiced flavour and will make it a great complement to pork or poultry. The cloves will rise to the top of the jelly and can easily be removed just before serving.*

Pour jelly into a sterilized jar, leaving ½ inch / 1 cm of headspace. Cool for 30 minutes. Pour a thin layer of hot paraffin wax over the jelly. Let harden, then add a second thin layer, rotating the glass to insure a tight seal. Cover, label and store in a cool, dry place.

MAKES 4 OR 5 8-OZ / 250-ML JARS.

Mint Jelly

4 LBS	GRANNY SMITH APPLES	2 KG
4 CUPS	WATER	1 L
	SUGAR, AS NEEDED	
1 CUP	FRESH MINT LEAVES	250 ML
¼ CUP	CIDER VINEGAR	50 ML
2 TBSP	SUGAR	30 ML

We prefer mint jelly to mint sauce with lamb. This recipe is not the insipid sweet mint jelly you might find in stores. Our mint jelly has the lovely fragrance and flavour of fresh mint and apples, plus the sharpness of vinegar found in mint sauce. If you have mint in your garden, turn some of this fragrant herb into jelly, especially for lamb dishes.

W & R

Wash apples and cut them in half. Place them in a large pot with a heavy bottom. Add water, cover and cook over medium heat for 30 to 35 minutes, until fruit is soft. Pour the contents of the pot into a jelly bag. Hang the jelly bag from a hook or a cupboard door handle overnight and allow juice to drip into a clean glass bowl. Dispose of pulp in the compost. For every cup of juice extracted, add ¾ cup / 175 ml sugar. Bring to a boil and simmer in the pot until juice tests for jelly. Meanwhile, wash and chop mint leaves. Combine mint, cider vinegar and sugar in a small pan. Simmer over medium heat for 2 minutes, remove from stove and let stand for one hour.

Add mint liquid to apple jelly mixture. Bring to a boil, skim off foam, pour into sterile glass jars and seal.

MAKES 4 TO 6 8-OZ / 250-ML JARS.

TIP: *When making jelly don't cut back on the sugar. The jam or jelly is likely to spoil.*

Lemon Curd

My mother had a hard time trying to convince me to taste lemon curd. She finally succeeded when I was in my teens. It was one of those "death by association" names that had me thinking that I couldn't possibly like it. Once you've tried it, I know that you will be hooked like me. Just imagine sitting down to a cup of tea and a plate of tiny pastry tarts filled with a light, lemony whip of sunshine.

R

3	EGGS, BEATEN	3
1 CUP	WHITE SUGAR	250 ML
½ CUP	LEMON JUICE	125 ML
¼ CUP	BUTTER OR MARGARINE	50 ML
1 Tbsp	LEMON RIND (ZEST), GRATED	15 ML

Mix all of the ingredients in small saucepan with a heavy bottom. Cook over low heat for 10 to 12 minutes, whisking constantly and keeping mixture just below boiling until it starts to thicken, or begins to coat spoon. Remove from heat and cool. Cover and refrigerate until ready to use.

Fill tiny baked pastry tart shells, use in **Picnic Lemon Roll** or spread it on toasted English muffins.

MAKES ABOUT 1½ CUPS / 750 ML.

TIP: *When using eggs, always break them into a separate bowl. Should there be a problem with the egg, you won't have to discard the entire recipe.*

1 CUP	SUGAR (LESS FOR MORE TART SAUCE)	250 ML
½ CUP	WATER	125 ML
1 TBSP	WORCESTERSHIRE SAUCE	15 ML
2 TBSP	BUTTER	30 ML
3 TBSP	RED WINE VINEGAR	45 ML
	SALT AND PEPPER TO TASTE	
	PINCH OF MACE	
¼ CUP	BLUEBERRIES	50 ML
	DASH OF TABASCO SAUCE	

PIQUANT BLUEBERRY SAUCE

We still pick wild blueberries on top of Pancake Hill on the old Gorham homestead, but there aren't enough for all the recipes we make at the Inn. We generally buy at least fifty pounds to keep in the freezer; that way, we know we'll have enough to take us from season to season.

W & R

Dissolve sugar in water in a saucepan over medium heat. Boil for about 5 minutes. Add Worcestershire sauce, butter, red wine vinegar, salt and pepper and mace, and simmer gently. Add blueberries and Tabasco, and heat, but do not boil. Serve over gently sautéed slices of pork tenderloin.

MAKES ABOUT 2 CUPS / 500 ML.

73
FROM THE
KITCHEN STOVE

CRANBERRY SAUCE

1 ½ CUPS	SUGAR	375 ML
1 ⅛ CUPS	WATER	280 ML
12 OZ	CRANBERRIES, FRESH OR FROZEN	340 G
	DASH OF SALT	

No turkey dinner is complete without cranberry sauce. In a pinch, we have settled for the commercial canned variety, but we prefer fresh sauce made the same day we cook the turkey. If we haven't managed to pick enough berries at our secret "bog" in October, we buy several bags when they are available in the supermarkets at a reasonable price and freeze them, just as they come, in 12-oz / 340-g bags. Then we're assured a good supply all winter when the prices are high or cranberries are unavailable.

W & R

Combine sugar and water in a saucepan, stirring over medium-high heat until sugar dissolves. Bring to a boil. Add cranberries and salt and boil without stirring until the skins on the berries start to pop (about 10 minutes).

Pour into prepared jars or directly into serving dishes. Cool before serving.

MAKES 3 CUPS / 750 ML.

1 TBSP	BUTTER	15 ML
1	ONION, FINELY CHOPPED	1
1	SMALL GREEN PEPPER, FINELY CHOPPED	1
1 CUP	CHICKEN STOCK	250 ML
3	TOMATOES, CHOPPED	3
½ TSP	SUGAR	2 ML
½ TSP	TABASCO SAUCE	2 ML
1 TBSP	FRESH SUMMER SAVORY, CHOPPED	15 ML
2 TSP	CORNSTARCH	10 ML
1 TBSP	WATER	15 ML

Spicy Tomato Sauce

A tangy accompaniment to fish or crab cakes, salmon loaf or fresh fish, this sauce is best eaten the day it's made, but it can be stored in the refrigerator for up to one week. Fresh tomatoes are best, but in the middle of winter, don't hesitate to use canned tomatoes.

W & R

Melt butter in a medium saucepan; add onion and pepper, and sauté for 2 minutes or until pepper is soft. Stir in chicken stock, tomatoes, sugar, Tabasco and savory. Bring to a boil, reduce heat and simmer, uncovered, for 15 minutes. Mix cornstarch and water in a small dish and stir into sauce. Heat, stirring constantly, until sauce boils and thickens. Serve hot as an accompaniment to your favourite seafood.

SERVES 4.

75
FROM THE
KITCHEN STOVE

Thick & Easy Hollandaise Sauce

This recipe alone is worth the price of the cookbook, in my humble opinion. After struggling to make Hollandaise sauce and finding it a long, arduous and often imperfect process, a friend gave me this wonderful microwave recipe. Try it.

R

¼ CUP	BUTTER OR MARGARINE	50 ML
2 TBSP	FRESH LEMON JUICE	30 ML
3	EGG YOLKS	3
¼ TSP	SALT	1 ML
	PINCH OF CAYENNE PEPPER	

Melt butter in a small glass bowl or baking dish at medium high in microwave oven for about 1 minute. Remove from microwave and beat in lemon juice, egg yolks and salt using wire whisk. Return to microwave and cook at medium heat for another 60 to 90 seconds, pausing every so often to whisk mixture and check on desired thickness. Add pinch of cayenne pepper and serve over vegetables, eggs or fish.

This is a guaranteed no-fail recipe that produces a wonderfully thick, creamy Hollandaise sauce, the envy of every cook. We hope you enjoy it.

MAKES ABOUT ½ CUP / 125 ML.

⅓ LB	BUTTER	150 G
1 TBSP	FRESH ROSEMARY, FINELY CHOPPED	15 ML
½ TSP	BLACK PEPPERCORNS, CRACKED	2 ML
2 TSP	LEMON RIND (ZEST), GRATED	10 ML

Place all ingredients in the small bowl of an electric mixer or a food processor; beat until combined. Spoon mixture onto a sheet of waxed paper, shape into a roll 2 inches / 5 cm in diameter and roll in paper, twisting ends to secure. Wrap in plastic wrap. Refrigerate until firm. Cut into thin ¼-inch / 5-mm slices and use as desired.

MAKES ⅓ LB / 150 G.

ROSEMARY-LEMON BUTTER

We have cut down on our butter consumption and now use a healthy margarine on toast and sandwiches. However, we still cook some dishes with butter and find there is no substitute for its flavour. This herb butter is lovely served with lamb, chicken or fish. It can be made two days ahead and, if properly wrapped, keeps well in refrigerator or freezer.

W&R

Appetizers, Soups
and Salads

Bacon-Nut Spread

4	SLICES BACON	4
¼ CUP	ALMONDS, TOASTED AND CHOPPED	50 ML
8 OZ	CREAM CHEESE, SOFTENED	225 G
¾ CUP	SOUR CREAM	175 ML
¼ CUP	ONION, MINCED	50 ML
¼ CUP	RED PEPPER, MINCED	50 ML
¼ TSP	SALT	1 ML
	PEPPER TO TASTE	

Fry bacon slices until they are brown and crisp. Cool, crumble and reserve. Drain off fat, then in same frying pan, toss almonds over medium heat until lightly toasted. Remove from heat, cool and chop finely. Mix cream cheese and sour cream in a glass bowl. Add crumbled bacon, almonds, onion, red pepper, salt and pepper. Stir well. Place in a suitable serving dish, cover and refrigerate. Remove from refrigerator about 15 minutes before serving. Remove crusts from slices of rye bread and cut each piece into 4 mini-slices. Serve with the spread.

MAKES 2 ½ CUPS / 725 ML.

Appetizers are wonderful beginnings to meals. They should whet, not dull, the appetite. Be careful not to allow your guests to fill up on canapés, or they will not be able to enjoy the sumptuous repast you have planned. Here's a savoury spread that is great on toast points or crackers.

W & R

81
TEASERS &
TEMPTERS

Salmon & Chive Cheese Spread

½ LB	COOKED OR CANNED SALMON	225 G
½ CUP	CREAM CHEESE, SOFTENED	125 ML
½ CUP	MAYONNAISE	125 ML
2 TBSP	LEMON JUICE	30 ML
1 TBSP	BUTTER, MELTED	15 ML
2 TBSP	FRESH CHIVES, CHOPPED	30 ML

Chives are the first herbs through the ground in the spring. By mid-April, we're picking them on the south side of the Inn. They're also easy to grow inside. Through the winter we have a small pot of chives in our window that we use sparingly, chopped and sprinkled over soups, or as a garnish. The small mauve flowers are edible, look nice on salads, and add colour to a plate of white fish.

W & R

Using a blender, mix undrained salmon, cheese, mayonnaise and lemon juice until well combined. With motor running, gradually add butter and process until smooth. Stir in chives. Pour mixture into serving dish and refrigerate until ready to serve. Serve with melba toast, crackers or as a spread on French bread. We sometimes put a small amount in individual dishes and serve as an appetizer with raw vegetables and crackers.

MAKES 2 CUPS / 500 ML.

Baked Sausage Cups

18	SLICES BREAD, 9 WHITE/9 BROWN	18
½ CUP	BUTTER, MELTED	125 ML
½ CUP	ONION, FINELY CHOPPED	125 ML
½ CUP	MUSHROOMS, CHOPPED	125 ML
1	CLOVE GARLIC, CRUSHED	1
¼ LB	SWEET SAUSAGE MEAT	115 G
¼ LB	HOT SAUSAGE MEAT	115 G
¼ TSP	THYME	1 ML
¼ TSP	OREGANO	1 ML
1 TBSP	ALL-PURPOSE FLOUR	15 ML
⅔ CUP	WHIPPING CREAM	150 ML
1 TBSP	LEMON JUICE	15 ML
	SALT AND PEPPER TO TASTE	
4 TBSP	PARMESAN CHEESE	60 ML

Here's a recipe for a hearty "man-size" hors d'oeuvre. These cups are best served hot from the oven, but the spicy sausage meat gives them a bite of their own, even when cold. Make them fancy (use a fluted knife to trim the crusts) or as rough as you wish (leave the bread untrimmed). The final result will bring raves no matter how much or how little you fuss.

W & R

PREHEAT OVEN TO 375° F / 190° C.

Cut crusts from bread slices. Roll slices with rolling pin to flatten. Press into greased muffin cups. Brush with butter and bake 6 to 8 minutes until browned. Cool and put back in muffin tins for filling.

Melt remaining butter in a frying pan over medium heat; sauté onion, mushrooms and garlic until soft. Stir in sausage meat and cook 8 or 10 minutes, until meat is well done. Whisk together thyme, oregano, flour, cream and lemon juice. Add to meat mixture. Stir until well mixed. Add salt and pepper to taste; spoon mixture into toasted cups. Sprinkle with Parmesan cheese and bake 6 to 8 minutes until hot.

Serve immediately.

MAKES 18 APPETIZERS.

Mini Drumsticks

A favourite at our "stand-up" receptions, these little drumsticks take a lot of time to prepare, so it's nice to have some help if you're getting ready for a crowd. We like to listen to lively music (something with a fiddle in it) and "have a visit" while we cook together in the kitchen. Preparation like this doesn't take a lot of thought, so you can have a stimulating conversation while you work.

W & R

2 LBS	CHICKEN WINGS	1 KG
¼ CUP	MAPLE SYRUP	50 ML
¼ CUP	SHERRY	50 ML
¼ CUP	LEMON JUICE	50 ML
2	CLOVES GARLIC, CHOPPED	2
1 TBSP	PAPRIKA	15 ML
1 TSP	LEMON RIND (ZEST), GRATED	5 ML
	PINCH OF CAYENNE	

Cut off wing tips and reserve for stock. Remove small bone from main wing section, using a small sharp knife. Cut meat around bone near joint and pull meat down like a stocking into a knob shape at the end. This leaves the bone sticking out as a handle. Place these mini drumsticks in a glass bowl.

Mix maple syrup, sherry, lemon juice, garlic, paprika, lemon zest and cayenne in a small saucepan. Place pan over medium heat and bring to a boil. Pour marinade over drumsticks in a glass bowl. Let stand several hours, or overnight, turning from time to time.

PREHEAT OVEN TO 375° F / 190° C.

Place chicken in a well-greased baking dish along with marinade. Bake about 40 minutes, basting often. Serve warm or cold. You can make these ahead of time and reheat them.

MAKES ABOUT 24 APPETIZERS.

FIDDLEHEADS IN PHYLLO

1 Tbsp	BUTTER	15 ml
1½ cups	ONION, CHOPPED	375 ml
¼ cup	RED PEPPER, CHOPPED	50 ml
1 Tbsp	CHEDDAR CHEESE, GRATED	50 ml
¼ cup	PARMESAN CHEESE, GRATED	50 ml
1 Tbsp	LEMON RIND (ZEST), GRATED	15 ml
1 tsp	LEMON JUICE	5 ml
1 Tbsp	FRESH DILL	15 ml
½ tsp	FRESHLY GROUND BLACK PEPPER	2 ml
	SALT TO TASTE	
8	SHEETS PHYLLO PASTRY, CUT IN HALF	8
¼ cup	BUTTER, MELTED	50 ml
½ lb	FIDDLEHEADS, LIGHTLY COOKED	225 g

As May approaches, we anxiously await the first fiddleheads in the Saint John City Market. For the next several weeks we buy or pick them as often as we can to be sure we've had our fill for another year. Even though we freeze them, we want to eat them fresh at least twice a week when they're in season. It's a bit of a fiddlehead feeding frenzy.

W & R

PREHEAT OVEN TO 375° F / 190° C.

Heat butter in a frying pan over medium heat and sauté onion and red pepper until soft. Cool. Mix with cheeses, lemon zest and juice, dill, pepper and salt, and set aside. Carefully lay down one half sheet of phyllo pastry, keeping the other sheets covered with a damp cloth to avoid drying out. Brush sheet of phyllo with butter and place several fiddleheads on pastry near one end. Place 1 Tbsp / 15 ml onion-cheese mixture on top of fiddleheads.

Fold both sides of phyllo over mixture and brush with butter. Carefully roll phyllo and fiddlehead mixture to form a packet. Brush with butter as you fold. Place on a baking sheet. Repeat with remaining sheets of phyllo.

Bake for 10 to 15 minutes until packets are nicely browned. Serve hot.

MAKES 16 APPETIZERS.

FIDDLEHEAD QUICHE APPETIZERS

When fiddleheads are plentiful, we have them as often as we can. It is possible to feature them for every course, except dessert, and we're working on that as well.

W & R

1 CUP	CHEDDAR CHEESE, GRATED	250 ML
24	UNBAKED TART SHELLS	24
1 LB	FIDDLEHEADS, FRESH OR FROZEN	450 G
½ LB	CREAM CHEESE, SOFTENED	225 G
¼ CUP	MILK	50 ML
4	EGGS	4
1 TBSP	CHIVES, CHOPPED	15 ML
1 TSP	SALT	5 ML
1 TBSP	PARMESAN CHEESE, GRATED	15 ML
	PAPRIKA	

PREHEAT OVEN TO 400° F / 200° C.

Sprinkle half the Cheddar cheese in tart shells. Place one whole cooked fiddlehead in each shell; coarsely chop the remaining fiddleheads, adding to the tart. In a bowl, combine softened cream cheese and milk until smooth. Add eggs, chives and salt; beat well. Spoon over fiddleheads. Cover with remaining Cheddar and Parmesan cheese. Sprinkle lightly with paprika.

Bake for 20 minutes or until set in center. Cool slightly before serving.

MAKES 24 SMALL QUICHES. SERVES 6 TO 8.

Mussels in Mushrooms

12	MUSSELS	12
2 TBSP	LEMON JUICE	30 ML
12	LARGE MUSHROOMS	12
1 TBSP	BUTTER OR VEGETABLE OIL	15 ML
1 TBSP	ONION, CHOPPED	15 ML
1 TSP	GARLIC, CHOPPED	5 ML
1 TSP	FRESH PARSLEY, CHOPPED	5 ML
1 TSP	FRESH DILL, CHOPPED	5 ML
4 TBSP	BREADCRUMBS	60 ML
	SALT AND PEPPER TO TASTE	
	DRY WHITE WINE TO MOISTEN	

PREHEAT OVEN TO 400° F / 200° C.

Steam mussels and remove from shells. Set aside.

Bring a saucepan of water to the boil; add lemon juice, and blanch mushrooms for about 1 minute. Drain and cool. Remove stems and centre stalk with a small spoon. Reserve caps and chop the stems.

Heat butter in a frying pan over medium heat; sauté mushroom pieces, onion, garlic, parsley, dill and breadcrumbs. Add salt and pepper to taste and enough white wine to moisten. Remove from heat. Lightly chop mussels and add to mixture with salt and pepper. Spoon into mushroom caps. Place on a tray and bake for 10 minutes.

SERVES 6.

There are still some mussel beds in the Maritimes where you can harvest wild mussels. If you do, you will have to be careful to wash and de-beard the shells before steaming and eating. Most of us simply go to the fish market and buy the commercially grown mussels, which only need a quick rinse before preparing. However, do be careful that the shells are tightly closed or close when touched. Always discard those that do not open when cooked.

W & R

Zucchini Frittata

People who have refused to eat zucchini, kids included, will gobble up this pizza-like frittata. Your neighbours, who have wheelbarrows of the oversized squash, will thank you for this recipe.

W & R

½ CUP	VEGETABLE OR OLIVE OIL	125 ML
4 CUPS	ZUCCHINI, SLICED	1 L
1 CUP	ONION, CHOPPED	250 ML
2	EGGS, WELL BEATEN	2
2 CUPS	MOZZARELLA CHEESE, GRATED	500 ML
½ CUP	FRESH PARSLEY, CHOPPED	125 ML
½ TSP	BASIL	2 ML
½ TSP	OREGANO	2 ML
½ TSP	SALT	2 ML
½ TSP	PEPPER	2 ML
½ TSP	GARLIC POWDER	2 ML

PREHEAT OVEN TO 375° F / 190° C.

Heat oil in a large non-stick frying pan over medium heat; sauté zucchini and onion until soft, about 10 minutes. Blend eggs and cheese in a large bowl. Add herbs, spices and vegetable mixture, and mix well. To serve as a luncheon dish, bake in a buttered quiche pan. If used as an appetizer, bake in an 8 ½ x 11-inch / 3-litre pan, and cut into bite-size squares or triangles. Bake for 20 minutes.

Cool 10 minutes before cutting. Serve warm.

MAKES 24 APPETIZERS.

SALMON MOUSSE

¼ CUP	COLD WATER	50 ML
1	ENVELOPE UNFLAVOURED GELATIN	1
½ CUP	BOILING WATER	125 ML
½ CUP	MAYONNAISE	125 ML
1 TBSP	LEMON OR LIME JUICE	15 ML
1 TBSP	ONION, GRATED	15 ML
⅛ TSP	HOT PEPPER SAUCE	.5 ML
1 TSP	SALT	5 ML
¼ CUP	FRESH DILL WEED, CHOPPED	50 ML
1 LB	SALMON, COOKED OR CANNED	450 G
1 CUP	WHIPPING CREAM	250 ML
¼ CUP	CAPERS, DRAINED	50 ML
	CHERRY TOMATOES, PARSLEY, LEMON WEDGES AND CRACKERS FOR GARNISHING	

A delicious hors d'oeuvre for that special occasion. It can be prepared the day before serving, and leftovers can be saved in the refrigerator for another day or two and served as a dip for the family. But don't count on there being any left.

W & R

Pour cold water into a large bowl and sprinkle with gelatin. Let stand for 5 minutes to soften. Add boiling water and stir until gelatin is dissolved; set aside to cool. Stir in mayonnaise, lemon juice, onion, hot sauce, salt and dill weed; mix until smooth and well combined. Refrigerate until slightly thickened, about 15 minutes.

Drain salmon and discard skin. Flake salmon and discard bones. Fold into gelatin mixture. Whip cream until soft peaks form. Fold into salmon, add capers and lightly blend. Pack into a 6-cup / 1.5-litre mould. Cover and refrigerate until firm (at least 4 hours).

Unmould onto a large serving dish and garnish with cherry tomatoes, parsley, lemon wedges and layers of crackers.

SERVES 24.

89
TEASERS &
TEMPTERS

Shrimp Kiev

A wonderful surprise awaits your guests when you serve this delectable appetizer. Hot herbed butter oozes onto their plates as they cut into the delicate, golden parcel, so serve warm bread or rolls to soak up the juices. If you make Shrimp Kiev ahead of time and cook the shrimp just before serving, the aroma will give your guests a hint of what is to follow.

W & R

½ CUP	BUTTER	125 ML
1	CLOVE GARLIC, CRUSHED	1
¼ CUP	FRESH PARSLEY, CHOPPED	50 ML
1 TBSP	DIJON MUSTARD	15 ML
½ TSP	HORSERADISH	2 ML
1 LB	FRESH SHRIMP, SHELLED (APPROXIMATELY 24)	450 G
	FLOUR FOR DREDGING	
2	EGGS, BEATEN, WITH A PINCH OF SALT	2
¼ CUP	MILK	50 ML
1 CUP	SEASONED BREADCRUMBS	250 ML
	VEGETABLE OIL FOR BROWNING	

Mix butter, garlic, parsley, mustard and horseradish in a small bowl until smooth. Form mixture into a roll about 1 inch / 2.5 cm thick by wrapping in aluminum foil and refrigerating for 1 hour or until firm. When solid, unwrap and cut into pieces about 1 ½ inches / 3.5 cm long.

Arrange 2 shrimp head to tail in a tight circle, on folded waxed paper. Carefully pound with a rolling pin to flatten into a cutlet shape. Wet your hands so shrimp won't stick to them, then form each shrimp cutlet around a piece of the herbed butter.

Roll shrimp parcel in flour. Mix egg and milk, and dip shrimp in mixture. Dredge in crumb mixture. Chill cutlets in refrigerator; fry in hot oil 2 to 3 minutes per side until golden brown.

Serve as a hot appetizer with **Seafood Cocktail Sauce** and garnish with lemon wedges.

MAKES 12 APPETIZERS.

¼ CUP	KETCHUP	50 ML
2 TSP	LEMON JUICE	10 ML
1 TSP	HORSERADISH	5 ML
¼ TSP	SALT	1 ML
	BLACK PEPPER, FRESHLY GROUND	
	FEW DROPS OF TABASCO SAUCE	
	FEW DROPS OF WORCESTERSHIRE SAUCE	

Seafood Cocktail Sauce

In small bowl, mix ingredients together. Season to taste, making the sauce as hot as you like. Keep refrigerated. Serve with steamed shrimp, mussels, clams or periwinkles.

MAKES ¼ CUP / 50 ML.

Most people are familiar with shrimp, mussels and clams, but not everyone has tried periwinkles. We ate a lot of them when I was a child. My brothers and I would head to the Bay of Fundy, pick periwinkles off the rocks and then take them back to Crystal Beach, where we'd steam them and offer them to our teenage friends. Some would walk away in disgust, but several would join us in removing the small morsel of tasty meat from the dull, gray shells.

W & R

CREAMY BAKED DIGBY SCALLOPS

1 LB	SCALLOPS	450 G
1 TBSP	BUTTER	15 ML
1 CUP	10% CREAM OR CANNED MILK	250 ML
	SALT AND PEPPER TO TASTE	
6	SODA CRACKERS, CRUSHED	6
½ CUP	CHEDDAR CHEESE, GRATED	125 ML
	LEMON WEDGES AND FRESH PARSLEY FOR GARNISHING	

Digby scallops are reputed to be the best in the world. We've eaten scallops throughout North America and we must agree: they are the best. Large, white, fresh creamy scallops from the Bay of Fundy can't be beaten. They should always be cooked when they are fresh and as little as possible. This easy recipe can be served as a light lunch with a salad and rolls or as an appetizer.

W&R

PREHEAT OVEN TO 375° F / 190° C.

Place scallops in a well-greased casserole dish and dot with butter. Cover with cream and sprinkle with salt and pepper, cracker crumbs and cheese. Bake 20 to 30 minutes, until top is browned and casserole bubbly.

Cool 10 minutes and serve garnished with lemon wedges and fresh parsley. These scallops are also delicious with fresh pasta or rice.

SERVES 4.

92
TEASERS & TEMPTERS

Smoked Eel in Phyllo Pastry with Mustard-Horseradish Sauce

2	SHEETS PHYLLO PASTRY	2
¼ CUP	MELTED BUTTER	60 ML
½	SMOKED EEL, SKINNED, BONED AND CUT INTO SERVING-SIZED PIECES	½

SAUCE

1 TBSP	BUTTER OR MARGARINE	15 ML
1 TBSP	FLOUR	15 ML
1 CUP	CHICKEN STOCK	250 ML
½ CUP	10% CREAM	125 ML
1 TBSP	DIJON MUSTARD	15 ML
1 TSP	HORSERADISH	5 ML
1 TSP	DRIED PARSLEY	5 ML

Eels are plentiful in our local rivers. Like all fatty fish, they lend themselves to smoking. If you have the opportunity, try them. Like us, you'll probably be pleasantly surprised.

W & R

PREHEAT OVEN TO 375° F / 190° C.

If using frozen phyllo pastry, defrost it in refrigerator overnight. Cover unused dough with a damp cloth. Open one sheet of pastry and brush with melted butter. Lay a second sheet over the first and brush with butter. Cut pastry sheet into 4 rectangular strips. Cover with a damp cloth.

Skin and bone eel and cut into four fillets. Cut fillets into serving size pieces that fit phyllo strips. Place piece of eel onto end of pastry. Fold side edges over full length of pastry strip, and brush with melted butter. Roll up each strip halfway and brush with melted butter. Continue rolling to end; brush packet with melted butter. Place packet seam down on greased baking sheet. Bake for 10 minutes or until golden brown.

Melt butter in a small frying pan over medium heat. Stir in flour; add chicken stock, letting mixture bubble. Turn down heat; mix in cream, mustard, horseradish and parsley, blending well. Cool slightly. Sauce should not be too thick. Drizzle sauce over warm eel packets and serve.

SERVES 4.

Clam Chowder

When we need lunch or a light supper and don't have a lot of time for preparation, we make clam chowder. You can always count on our cupboard having a few cans of baby clams and evaporated milk. Add potatoes and onion and it's ready to eat. It's that easy, and oh, so good.

W&R

4	SLICES BACON, FINELY DICED	4
½ CUP	ONION, FINELY CHOPPED	125 ML
2 CUPS	POTATO, PEELED AND DICED	500 ML
¼ CUP	CELERY, FINELY CHOPPED	50 ML
1 CUP	BOILING WATER	250 ML
2 5-OZ CANS	BABY CLAMS, UNDRAINED	2 142-G CANS
2½ CUPS	MILK, CANNED OR FRESH	625 ML
1 TSP	SALT	5 ML
⅛ TSP	PEPPER	.5 ML
¼ TSP	PAPRIKA	1 ML
¼ CUP	FRESH PARSLEY, CHOPPED	50 ML
2 TBSP	BUTTER	30 ML

Fry bacon until crisp in a heavy saucepan. Drain on a paper towel; set aside. Measure 2 Tbsp / 30 ml bacon fat into a large saucepan. Add onion; cook over medium heat until transparent, but do not brown. Add potato, celery, juice from clams and hot water. Bring to a boil, reduce heat, cover and cook until potatoes are tender, about 10 minutes. Add clams, milk, seasoning and butter. Stir well and heat thoroughly, but do not boil. Serve in individual bowls and garnish with bacon bits.

SERVES 4 TO 6.

Downeast Seafood Chowder

5-OZ CAN	BABY CLAMS	142-G CAN
1 CUP	LOBSTER, SHRIMP AND/OR SALMON	250 ML
½ TSP	SALT	2 ML
3	POTATOES, PEELED AND CUBED	3
1	CARROT, PEELED AND CUBED	1
1	SMALL ONION, FINELY CHOPPED	1
1	CELERY STALK, FINELY CHOPPED	1
¼ CUP	FRESH PARSLEY, CHOPPED	50 ML
½ LB	HADDOCK OR ANY WHITE FISH	225 G
½ LB	BROKEN SCALLOPS	225 G
1 TBSP	ALL-PURPOSE FLOUR	15 ML
½ TSP	PAPRIKA	2 ML
½ TSP	SALT	2 ML
⅛ TSP	PEPPER	5 ML
2 TBSP	VEGETABLE OIL OR BUTTER	30 ML
12-OZ CAN	EVAPORATED MILK	385-ML CAN
	OR	
2 CUPS	LIGHT CREAM OR WHOLE MILK	500 ML
1 TBSP	BUTTER	15 ML
	SALT AND PEPPER TO TASTE	
	DULSE FLAKES	

I've stopped ordering chowder when I'm not in the Maritimes. It's not that I'm fussy, but when you've had the best, it's difficult to settle for the rest. Maybe it's because we've always had easy access to lots of seafood, but our chowders remind me of the hamburger ad that claims "More Beef Than Bun." Chowders that are high in flour or artificial thickeners and low in seafood and cream just don't make it. Give this one a try. You'll know what I mean.

W

95
TEASERS &
TEMPTERS

Drain juice from clams and lobster into a large, heavy pot. Add enough water to make 2 cups. Add salt and potatoes, carrot, onion, celery and parsley. Cook until tender, about 10 minutes. Cut haddock into bite-size pieces. Mix flour, paprika, salt and pepper together. Lightly dust haddock and scallops (and shrimp or salmon, if used) with flour mixture; sauté in a frying pan of heated oil or butter. Add to vegetables along with other seafood. Heat milk in microwave and stir into fish mixture with butter. Add salt and pepper to taste. Heat through, but do not boil. Sprinkle with dulse flakes and serve.

SERVES 6 TO 8.

TIP: *To thicken soup or chowder, grate in fresh potato.*

Corn Chowder

Corn chowder has always been a staple in Maritime kitchens. It's often featured in small diners and is now showing up in larger restaurants. I've always enjoyed it, but never so much as when I was sailing through Europe, deprived of peanut butter, canned baked beans and corn. We arrived in Gibraltar to find all three items in a small English supermarket. Europeans, it seems, considered corn something fit for cattle, not humans. The can, from Windsor, Ontario, was labelled "A New Vegetable Product from Canada."

W

1 TBSP	BUTTER OR VEGETABLE OIL	15 ML
1	SMALL ONION, FINELY CHOPPED	1
1 CUP	BOILING WATER	250 ML
3	POTATOES, PEELED AND CUT INTO ½-INCH / 1-CM PIECES	3
1	STALK CELERY, FINELY CHOPPED	1
19-OZ CAN	CREAMED CORN	540-ML CAN
3 CUPS	MILK OR 10% CREAM	750 ML
1 TSP	SALT	5 ML
¼ TSP	PEPPER	1 ML
	BACON BITS OR BUTTER AND PAPRIKA FOR GARNISHING	

Melt butter in a large, heavy saucepan and add onion; sauté until transparent, but not brown. Add boiling water, potato and celery. Bring to a boil; reduce heat, cover and cook until tender, about 10 minutes. Add corn and milk. Season with salt and pepper. Heat but do not boil. Serve garnished with bacon bits if desired or a teaspoon of butter and paprika.

SERVES 6.

CREAMY SMOKED COD CHOWDER

6	SLICES BACON	6
3 TBSP	VEGETABLE OIL	45 ML
1	ONION, CHOPPED	1
1	CARROT, CHOPPED	1
1	CELERY RIB, CHOPPED	1
2 TBSP	ALL-PURPOSE FLOUR	30 ML
1 CUP	WATER	250 ML
3	POTATOES, PEELED AND CUT INTO 1-INCH / 2.5-CM CUBES	3
1 LB	SMOKED COD, CUT INTO ¾-INCH CHUNKS	450 G
1 TSP	SALT	5 ML
¼ TSP	PEPPER	1 ML
2 CUPS	EVAPORATED MILK OR 10% CREAM	500 ML
	CHEDDAR CHEESE, GRATED	

Although all chowders don't contain fish, the name does originate from the French *chaudière*, a cauldron in which fishermen made their stews fresh from the sea. When we were growing up, our parents often served smoked or dried salt cod because we didn't have proper refrigeration. Smoked cod is still available and is exquisite in this chowder.

W & R

Cut bacon into ½ inch / 1 cm squares and fry over medium-high heat until crisp on both sides, 4 to 6 minutes. Drain on paper towels. Heat 3 Tbsp / 45 ml vegetable oil (or 1 Tbsp / 15 ml bacon fat mixed with 2 Tbsp / 30 ml vegetable oil) in a large, heavy pot. Add onion, carrot and celery. Cook, stirring often, for 4 to 6 minutes, until softened. Blend in flour and stir for an additional 2 minutes. Pour in water and bring to a boil. Add potatoes, fish, salt and pepper. Cover and continue cooking for 10 to 12 minutes on medium-high, until potatoes are tender. Heat cream in a separate saucepan until hot but not boiling, and add to potato mixture. Sprinkle with bacon, simmer for 1 minute and serve. Garnish each bowl with grated Cheddar cheese.

SERVES 6 AS A FIRST COURSE, OR 3 AS A LIGHT LUNCH.

CREAM OF MUSSEL SOUP

This rich, creamy soup is a meal in itself if served in a large bowl. So if you plan to serve your guests another course, be sure to give them just a cup, even though they might ask for more.

W & R

2 LBS	FRESH CULTIVATED MUSSELS	900 G
2 TBSP	BUTTER	30 ML
1	ONION, CHOPPED	1
2 TBSP	PARSLEY, CHOPPED	30 ML
1	BAY LEAF	1
1 TSP	MARJORAM	5 ML
1 TBSP	THYME	15 ML
1½ CUPS	DRY WHITE WINE	375 ML
1 CUP	CHICKEN BROTH	250 ML
2	EGG YOLKS	2
2 CUPS	18% CREAM	500 ML
	SALT AND PEPPER TO TASTE	
	CHOPPED CHIVES FOR GARNISHING	

Rinse mussels with fresh water. Meanwhile, in a shallow pan or Dutch oven, melt butter and briefly simmer onion, parsley, bay leaf, marjoram and thyme. Add live mussels and white wine. Cover and simmer for five minutes or longer, until all shells have opened. Strain mussels using a sieve. Reserve broth. Remove meat from shells and reserve.

Simmer mussel broth along with chicken stock in a large, heavy saucepan. In a separate bowl, whisk egg yolks, adding broth while whisking rapidly. Return mixture to stove and bring almost to a boil. Whisk in cream and adjust salt and pepper to taste. Remove from heat, add mussel meat and serve piping hot in bowls. Garnish with chopped chives. Serve with crusty rolls.

SERVES 4.

TIP: *Preparing mussels takes some care. After scrubbing and rinsing, trim off beards with scissors. Discard mussels that have damaged shells or are open. If you're uncertain about a mussel that is partially open, tap it lightly and discard if it doesn't close. After cooking, discard any mussels that haven't opened. The cultivated mussels currently available are very clean and take less time to prepare.*

Dulse Soup

2 Tbsp	BUTTER OR MARGARINE	30 ML
1	SMALL ONION, CHOPPED	1
4 CUPS	MILK OR 10% CREAM	1 L
1½ CUPS	MASHED POTATOES	375 ML
1 Tbsp	DULSE FLAKES	15 ML
1 TSP	WORCESTERSHIRE SAUCE	5 ML

Melt butter in a medium saucepan and sauté onion over medium heat until slightly browned. Add milk and mashed potatoes, stirring well. Add dulse flakes and stir while bringing the soup almost to a boil. Add Worcestershire sauce to taste.

SERVES 4.

I was introduced to dulse some years ago, when I first visited New Brunswick. I immediately acquired a taste for the salty seaweed. I had grown to like nori, a Pacific Coast seaweed cousin, used in many Japanese sushi dishes. We now use dulse in many of our seafood recipes. It provides a wonderful briny flavour and a colourful accent to several dishes. Here's a recipe you must try. If you like dulse, you'll love this soup.

R

99
TEASERS &
TEMPTERS

FIDDLEHEADS & CREAM SOUP

Nothing compares to the taste of fresh fiddleheads after a long cold winter and a damp, wet April.

W&R

2 CUPS	FIDDLEHEADS, CLEANED AND CHOPPED	500 ML
½ TSP	SALT	2 ML
1 CUP	WATER	250 ML
2 CUPS	CHICKEN STOCK	500 ML
1	LARGE POTATO, PEELED AND DICED	1
1	ONION, DICED	1
1	BAY LEAF	1
1 TBSP	BUTTER	15 ML
1 CUP	10% CREAM OR MILK	250 ML
	SALT AND PEPPER TO TASTE	
	LEMON RIND (ZEST), GRATED	
	DULSE FLAKES TO TASTE (OPTIONAL)	

Cook fiddleheads in 1 cup / 250 ml salted water in a large saucepan until tender, about 4 to 5 minutes. Drain, reserve greens and cool slightly; coarsely chop.

Combine water, chicken stock, diced potato, onion and bay leaf in a large, heavy saucepan. Boil for 8 to 10 minutes, until potato is tender. Remove and discard bay leaf. Mix in butter. Add half the chopped fiddlehead greens and process mixture in blender until smooth, adding cream for desired consistency.

Return to saucepan, place over medium heat and gently stir in remainder of chopped fiddleheads while reheating. Add salt and pepper to taste. Serve hot and steamy, with a light sprinkling of grated lemon zest and dulse flakes.

SERVES 4 TO 6.

100
TEASERS &
TEMPTERS

¼ CUP	ONION, DICED	50 ML
½ CUP	CELERY, DICED	125 ML
½ CUP	CARROT, SLICED	125 ML
½ CUP	FRESH PARSLEY SPRIGS	125 ML
1 CUP	WATER	250 ML
2 TBSP	DRIED CHICKEN BOUILLON	30 ML
1½ CUPS	TOMATO JUICE	375 ML
1 TSP	SUGAR	5 ML
1 TSP	WORCESTERSHIRE SAUCE	5 ML
1	BAY LEAF	1
	SALT AND PEPPER TO TASTE	

Put prepared vegetables, water, bouillon and juice into blender and set at grate (or the equivalent) for about 5 seconds, or until vegetables have become small grated chunks. Pour into a saucepan; add sugar, Worcestershire sauce and bay leaf. Simmer for 10 minutes or until hot. Season to taste. Remove and discard bay leaf and serve.

SERVES 4.

Fresh Vegetable Soup

We had guests arrive early for dinner one night. They had just flown from Europe and were tired and hungry. We sat them down in front of a blazing open fire and presented them with a smoked salmon appetizer and a glass of cold beer. While they enjoyed our first offering, we sprang into action and produced this soup for the second course. That's how quickly it can be made. And the flavour . . . well, try it.

W&R

TIP: *If you don't have a blender, you can chop the onion, celery and parsley and grate the carrot by hand.*

Herbed Zucchini Soup

Our good neighbours Bonnie and Greg have a wonderful vegetable garden they generously share with us. Avid gardeners, they plant more than they could ever eat. Naturally, there is always an abundance of zucchini and they count on us to take several of them off their hands, but they also appreciate any recipes we can find for this delicate squash. This soup is especially good as it can be frozen for two months.

W & R

1 Tbsp	BUTTER	15 ML
1 Tbsp	VEGETABLE OIL	15 ML
1	ONION, CHOPPED	1
2	CLOVES GARLIC, CHOPPED	2
6	ZUCCHINI, FINELY CHOPPED	6
3 CUPS	CHICKEN STOCK	750 ML
2 TSP	SUGAR	10 ML
1 Tbsp	LEMON JUICE	15 ML
⅓ CUP	FRESH BASIL, CHOPPED	75 ML
½ CUP	SOUR CREAM	125 ML
	PAPRIKA AND BASIL LEAVES	
	FOR GARNISHING	

Heat butter and oil in a saucepan; sauté onion and garlic over medium heat until onion is soft, about 2 minutes. Stir in zucchini, stock, sugar and lemon juice. Bring to a boil, reduce heat and simmer, uncovered, for 20 minutes, until zucchini is tender. Add basil.

Blend or process mixture in small batches until smooth. Return mixture to pan; reheat. Serve, adding a spoonful of sour cream to the centre of the soup. Sprinkle with paprika and garnish the sour cream with basil leaves.

SERVES 4.

PICNIC COLESLAW

3 LBS	CABBAGE	1.5 KG
2 LBS	CARROTS	1 KG
2	ONIONS	2
½ CUP	SUGAR	125 ML
1 CUP	WHITE VINEGAR	250 ML
1 CUP	VEGETABLE OIL	250 ML
1 CUP	WHITE SUGAR	250 ML
2 TSP	CELERY SEED	10 ML
1½ TSP	SALT	7 ML

Shred vegetables, sprinkle with sugar and toss.

Bring the vinegar, sugar, celery seed and salt to a boil in a saucepan over medium-high heat. Pour boiling liquid over vegetables. Pack in sealer jars and refrigerate. This coleslaw will keep for several weeks, if refrigerated.

MAKES ABOUT 20 CUPS / 5 LITRES.

We enjoy picnics any time of the year. They're a good excuse for families to get together. We plan picnics around any occasion: gathering wild berries, checking out good fishing locations, cross-country skiing or just walking the dog. We especially like this coleslaw because there is no mayonnaise, so it's not affected by lack of refrigeration.
W & R

TIP: *We always find the cup equivalent helpful if we are unsure of weight of veggies on hand. It's far clearer. 3 lbs / 1.5 kg of cabbage should produce approximately 12 cups / 3 litres of shredded cabbage; 2 lbs / 1 kg of carrots should render approximately 6 cups / 1.5 litres of shredded carrots.*

CREAMY COLESLAW

My father declared this the "World's Greatest Coleslaw." Dad didn't give compliments lightly, so I assumed it was. Now Ross has made the same declaration.

W

2 CUPS	CABBAGE, SHREDDED	500 ML
1	LARGE CARROT, GRATED	1
2 TSP	ONION, FINELY CHOPPED	10 ML
¼ TSP	GARLIC, CHOPPED	1 ML
1 TSP	LEMON JUICE	5 ML
3 TBSP	MAYONNAISE	45 ML
	SALT AND PEPPER TO TASTE	

Mix cabbage, carrot and onion in a large bowl. Stir in the rest of the ingredients. Place in the refrigerator until ready to serve.

Serve as a side dish by placing a crisp lettuce leaf in a small salad bowl and fill with coleslaw. Decorate with a tomato wedge or a slice of cucumber. Delicious as a leftover, creamy coleslaw will keep in the refrigerator for up to 3 days.

SERVES 6.

2 TBSP	GELATIN	30 ML
1 CUP	WATER	250 ML
2 TBSP	DRIED BEEF BOUILLON	30 ML
½ LB	CREAM CHEESE, SOFTENED	220 G
½ CUP	LIGHT MAYONNAISE	125 ML
1 CUP	PLAIN, LOW-FAT YOGURT	250 ML
¼ CUP	LEMON JUICE	50 ML
1 TSP	FRESHLY GROUND BLACK PEPPER	5 ML
1 TBSP	LEMON RIND (ZEST), GRATED	15 ML
¼ CUP	FRESH WATERCRESS, CHOPPED	50 ML
½ CUP	CARROT, FINELY GRATED	125 ML
1 CUP	ZUCCHINI, FINELY GRATED	250 ML
	WATERCRESS FOR GARNISHING	

MOULDED WATERCRESS SALAD

Watercress grows wild on river banks and is also grown commercially. You should be able to pick it up at your local supermarket. It has a sharp, peppery flavour and adds a hot spiciness to salads and sandwiches. Serve this salad as an appetizer or as an accompaniment to meat or fish. It's as colourful as it is flavourful.

W & R

In a small bowl, sprinkle gelatin over water and beef bouillon. Place bowl in a shallow pan of simmering water and stir until dissolved; cool slightly. Beat together cheese, mayonnaise and yogurt in the bowl of an electric mixer until smooth. Stir in lemon juice, ground pepper, lemon rind, watercress and gelatin mixture. Pour one-third of mixture into a lightly oiled 6-cup / 1.5-litre mould; refrigerate until set.

Spoon grated carrot into mould, leaving a ½-inch / 1-cm border around edges. Spread with half the remaining gelatin mixture and fill in borders; refrigerate until set.

Squeeze moisture from zucchini and spoon into mould, once again leaving a border around the edge. Spread with remaining gelatin mixture, filling around edges; refrigerate until set.

Turn mould onto plate and cut into slices. Garnish with watercress.

SERVES 8.

Marinated Salad

This favourite summer salad is great when your neighbour invites you to a barbecue and you offer to take something along.

W & R

1 CUP	VEGETABLE OIL	250 ML
½ CUP	WHITE VINEGAR	125 ML
¼ CUP	PARMESAN CHEESE, GRATED	50 ML
½ TSP	SALT	2 ML
¼ TSP	CELERY SALT	1 ML
½ TSP	PEPPER, FRESHLY GROUND	2 ML
½ TSP	DRY MUSTARD	2 ML
¼ TSP	PAPRIKA	1 ML
1	CLOVE GARLIC, MINCED	1
6	ARTICHOKE HEARTS (PACKED IN WATER)	6
3	SLICES THURINGER SAUSAGE (SALAMI)	3
12	CHERRY TOMATOES	12
1 CUP	FRESH MUSHROOMS	250 ML
½	GREEN PEPPER	½
½	RED PEPPER	½
6	GREEN ONIONS	6
1 TSP	CAPERS	5 ML
1	HEAD ROMAINE	1
1	BUNCH ARUGULA	1
	CROUTONS	
	PARMESAN CHEESE	

In a blender or mixer, beat together the oil, vinegar, Parmesan cheese, salt, celery salt, pepper, mustard, paprika and garlic. Set aside.

Cut artichoke hearts in quarters; slice thuringer into narrow strips; cut tomatoes in half; thinly slice mushrooms; cut peppers into strips and chop green onions, omitting the green tops. Toss with the marinade and add capers. Refrigerate in a covered bowl at least 2 hours or overnight.

Wash romaine, break into large pieces, and dry the lettuce in salad spinner. Wash and dry arugula, and arrange lettuces on individual plates; spoon well-drained marinated ingredients onto lettuce. Add several croutons to each salad and sprinkle with Parmesan. Serve with freshly ground pepper and hot rolls or French bread as an appetizer or a light lunch.

SERVES 4 TO 6.

¼ CUP	VEGETABLE OIL	50 ML
¼ CUP	LEMON JUICE	50 ML
1 TSP	SUGAR	5 ML
1 TBSP	HONEY	15 ML
2 TBSP	FRESH MINT, CHOPPED	30 ML
1 TSP	FRESHLY GROUND BLACK PEPPER	5 ML
2 LB	ZUCCHINI (6 TO 8)	900 G
1	RED PEPPER	1
	MINT LEAVES FOR GARNISHING	

MINTED ZUCCHINI SALAD

Combine the oil, lemon juice, sugar, honey, mint and pepper in a jar and shake well, or place the ingredients in a blender and blend for 10 seconds. Store in a refrigerator for up to 3 days ahead.

Using a vegetable peeler, peel thin strips from zucchini. Finely chop red pepper and mix with zucchini in a large bowl; add dressing and toss lightly.

Garnish salad with fresh mint leaves. Serve immediately.

SERVES 6.

In August, ask gardeners what they'd most like to give away and the answer will be zucchini. Ask them what perennial causes them the most grief and they'll say mint. One zucchini plant can often produce more squash than a family of four can consume, and one mint root can take over a small flower bed in a season. What better recipe than one that uses both zucchini and mint?

W & R

Quick Four- Bean Salad

We know it's best to eat fresh vegetables whenever we can, but there are times when we want to make something quickly. We really enjoy this bean salad, and we make it even when beans aren't in season. It keeps well in the refrigerator, and everyone likes it. Don't argue with success, just enjoy it.

W & R

½ CUP	WHITE VINEGAR	125 ML
¼ CUP	VEGETABLE OIL	50 ML
2 TBSP	WHITE SUGAR	30 ML
1 TSP	SALT	5 ML
	DASH OF PEPPER	
1	CLOVE GARLIC, CHOPPED	1
½ CUP	CELERY, SLICED	125 ML
¼ CUP	ONION, FINELY SLICED	50 ML
14-OZ CAN	GREEN BEANS	398-ML CAN
14-OZ CAN	YELLOW BEANS	398-ML CAN
14-OZ CAN	LIMA BEANS	398-ML CAN
14-OZ CAN	KIDNEY BEANS	398-ML CAN

Whisk together vinegar, oil, sugar, salt, pepper and garlic in a large glass bowl. Add celery, onion and drained beans. Toss well. Cover and refrigerate for 3 hours or overnight, stirring occasionally. Serve on fresh lettuce.

SERVES 8 TO 10.

1 LB	FRESH SQUID	450 G
1 TSP	VEGETABLE OIL	5 ML
1	SMALL ONION, CHOPPED	1
2	CLOVES GARLIC, CRUSHED	2
2	SMALL FRESH TOMATOES, CHOPPED	2
½ TSP	BASIL	2 ML
½ TSP	CHILI PEPPER	2 ML
4-OZ CAN	TOMATO SAUCE	120-G CAN
⅓ CUP	CHICKEN STOCK	75 ML
1 TSP	HONEY	5 ML
	BLACK OLIVES	

Squid Jiggers Salad

Squid is fished on both coasts of Canada and is readily available throughout the year. It's very popular in Japanese sushi bars, but is normally served deep-fried in North America.

W & R

Clean squid, reserving hoods. Slice hoods into rings. Bring 2 cups / 500 ml water to a boil in a saucepan. Add squid rings; cook about 45 seconds, until rings are opaque.

Rinse rings in cold water and reserve. Heat oil in a frying pan over medium heat; sauté chopped onion and garlic. Add chopped tomatoes, basil and chili pepper, stirring while cooking. Mix in tomato sauce, chicken stock and honey, and bring to a boil. Reduce heat; simmer until thickened.

Remove from heat, add black olives and cool. Before serving, add squid rings and stir well. Serve over a bed of lettuce and cucumber slices.

SERVES 4 TO 6.

109
TEASERS &
TEMPTERS

Spinach Salad with Tangy House Dressing

Popeye was right: spinach really is good for you. It's high in iron as well as vitamins A and C. Children often don't care for the texture of cooked spinach, but they will enjoy it in a salad. Raw vegetables are better for you anyway, so try this salad with your family.

W&R

6 CUPS	FRESH SPINACH, ROMAINE OR BIBB LETTUCE	1.5 L
1	RED ONION, FINELY SLICED	1
2 TBSP	RED WINE VINEGAR	30 ML
½ TSP	BROWN SUGAR	2 ML
2 TSP	DIJON MUSTARD	10 ML
⅓ CUP	VEGETABLE OR OLIVE OIL	75 ML
½ CUP	PINE NUTS OR PECANS, CHOPPED	125 ML
	SALT AND PEPPER TO TASTE	

Wash spinach and remove large, coarse stems from leaves. Tear leaves into bite-sized pieces. Wash and dry leaves in salad spinner. Toss red onion with spinach in a large bowl. In a small bowl, beat wine vinegar together with vegetable oil until rich and creamy; add brown sugar and Dijon mustard, continue beating until sugar is dissolved and mixture is emulsified. Add salt and pepper to taste.

Drizzle dressing over spinach and onion and sprinkle with pine nuts or chopped pecans.

SERVES 4 TO 6.

½ CUP	WINE VINEGAR	125 ML
2 TBSP	DIJON MUSTARD	30 ML
1½ TSP	SALT	7 ML
	FRESHLY GROUND PEPPER	
2	CLOVES GARLIC, CRUSHED	2
1½ CUPS	VEGETABLE OR OLIVE OIL	375 ML
2 TBSP	FRESH BASIL, CHOPPED	30 ML
1 LB	FIDDLEHEADS	450 G

FIDDLEHEADS IN BASIL VINAIGRETTE

Traditionally, fiddleheads were steamed or boiled and eaten with butter, salt and pepper. We still enjoy them like that, although we add a bit of fresh lemon. This pickled version is great as an accompaniment to smoked salmon, tossed into salads or served with sandwiches.

W & R

Mix all ingredients except fiddleheads in a blender; blend at high speed until well mixed. Makes 2 cups / 500 ml vinaigrette.

Clean fiddleheads and blanch them in boiling water for 1 to 2 minutes. Remove from hot water and plunge into ice-cold water. Once cooled, drain and mix with vinaigrette. Store in clean glass jars.

This vinaigrette also makes a tangy house dressing for general use. It will keep in the refrigerator for up to two weeks.

MAKES 3 TO 4 8-OZ / 250-ML JARS.

111
TEASERS &
TEMPTERS

TIP: *Keep marinated fiddleheads refrigerated for about one week before using.*

Classic Mixed Greens Dressing

Remember when salad dressings were either homemade mayonnaise or oil and vinegar? Mum used to mix sugar and vinegar to use on fresh lettuce from our garden. Now there are more varieties available than our mothers ever could have imagined, but we still prefer our own homemade versions.

W

¼ CUP	WINE VINEGAR	50 ML
1 TSP	DIJON MUSTARD	5 ML
1 TSP	LIQUID HONEY	5 ML
	SALT TO TASTE	
	FRESHLY GROUND BLACK PEPPER TO TASTE	
⅔ CUP	VEGETABLE OIL	150 ML
1 TBSP	FRESH HERBS (TARRAGON, PARSLEY, CHIVES)	15 ML

Whisk together all of the ingredients in a bowl, or use a blender for a creamier dressing. Refrigerate and use with your favourite green salad.

MAKES ABOUT ¾ CUP / 175 ML.

3 CUPS	OLIVE OIL	750 ML
5	SPRIGS FRESH OREGANO	5
2	CLOVES GARLIC, PEELED	2
8	WHOLE BLACK PEPPERCORNS	8
2	BAY LEAVES	2

Pour oil into jar. Arrange herbs decoratively in oil, put on lid or cork. Refrigerate.

MAKES 3 CUPS / 750 ML.

OREGANO HERBED OIL

Herb oil can be used in salad dressings or to add a subtle spicy flavour to fried dishes. The flavour improves if you let the oil rest for several days. Be sure to store oil in the refrigerator, and it will be good for about a month. Attractive glass bottles are available at most specialty stores and are quite inexpensive. Fill them, add a plaid ribbon to the top and give your herb oil to friends. They'll be quite impressed.

W & R

Tarragon Vinegar

4 CUPS	WHITE WINE VINEGAR	1 L
10	SPRIGS FRESH TARRAGON	10
10	WHOLE BLACK PEPPERCORNS	10
3	CLOVES GARLIC, PEELED	3

Vinegar will keep in jars in a cool, dark place for three months. Herb vinegars add a nice, subtle flavour to home-made salad dressings and vinaigrettes. They also make good housewarming or hostess gifts. We buy inexpensive cruets at our local dollar stores, add a label to the bottom of the cruet before filling and tie a piece of the dried herb to the handle with a rough piece of garden string.

W&R

Combine vinegar, half the tarragon, peppercorns and garlic in a large bowl. Let stand overnight in a warm place or until tarragon loses its colour; strain. Place remaining tarragon in jars, top with vinegar.

MAKES 4 CUPS / 1 LITRE.

Main Dishes
from
Land & Sea

1 LB	MEDIUM GROUND BEEF	450 G
12 TO 14	SODA CRACKERS, CRUSHED	125 ML
1	EGG	1
½ CUP	MILK	125 ML
1	SMALL ONION, FINELY CHOPPED	50 ML
¼ CUP	KETCHUP	50 ML
1 TSP	WORCESTERSHIRE SAUCE	5 ML
½ TSP	SALT	2 ML
¼ TSP	FRESHLY GROUND BLACK PEPPER	1 ML
¼ TSP	GARLIC, CRUSHED	1 ML

*M*ARITIME *M*EATLOAF

It took several attempts before Ross ate my meatloaf. Every time I would suggest it for dinner, he'd quickly prepare something else. Finally, one day when I was at home alone, I made it, along with baked potatoes and several of our favourite root vegetables. Ross tried it, loved it and looks forward to it now as much as I do.

W

PREHEAT OVEN TO 350° F / 180° C.

*M*ix all ingredients in a large bowl until mixture is quite moist, adding extra milk if necessary. Put in a greased loaf pan and bake 45 minutes, or until meat shrinks away from the pan. Cool for 10 minutes. Slice and serve.

Serve warm with baked potato or cold on sandwiches or with potato salad.

SERVES 4.

Cabbage Rolls

The first cabbage rolls we ever tried were quite bland and uninspiring. We enjoy cabbage rolls today because we've added a little snap to the traditional recipe.

W&R

1	LARGE HEAD GREEN CABBAGE	1

Sauce

16 OZ CAN	TOMATO SAUCE	450 ML CAN
¼ CUP	LEMON JUICE	50 ML
1	LARGE TOMATO, FINELY CHOPPED	1
⅓ CUP	BROWN SUGAR	75 ML
¼ TSP	PEPPER	1 ML

Filling

1 LB	GROUND BEEF	450 G
¾ CUP	RICE	175 ML
½ CUP	WATER, LIGHTLY SALTED	375 ML
1	LARGE ONION, FINELY CHOPPED	1
3	EGGS, BEATEN	3
1 TBSP	WORCESTERSHIRE SAUCE	15 ML
½ TSP	FRESHLY GROUND BLACK PEPPER	2 ML
¼ TSP	ALLSPICE	1 ML
1	CLOVE GARLIC, FINELY CHOPPED	1
½ CUP	TOMATO JUICE OR WATER	125 ML

PREHEAT OVEN TO 350° F / 180° C.

Cut ½ inch off the base of cabbage, to help free leaves as they are cooked. Place cabbage in about 3 quarts / 3 litres water in a large saucepan; bring to a boil. Sprinkle a small amount of salt over cabbage. Cover and simmer 20 or 25 minutes. Remove cabbage, reserving water if more cooking is needed. Cool cabbage slightly. Carefully remove the overlapping leaves from the head. They should be quite soft and pliable. If the last half of the cabbage is still too firm and the leaves won't remove easily, return it to the simmering pan of water for another 5 minutes or until leaves are softened. If some of the leaves you've removed are still too firm to roll up without breaking, return the leaves to pan with the cabbage for a couple of minutes.

Mix all ingredients for tomato sauce in a bowl and set aside.

Cook rice in salted water for 18 minutes.

Combine beef, rice, onion, eggs, Worcestershire sauce, pepper, allspice, garlic and tomato juice in a large bowl and mix well. Place about ⅛ cup / 25 ml of meat mixture onto a cabbage leaf; fold over sides of leaf and roll from the thicker stalk end to form a cigar-shaped packet. Repeat until all of the mixture is used.

Lightly oil the inside of an oven-proof casserole or Dutch oven. Add a small amount of tomato sauce. Place rolled cabbage packets into casserole, seamside down. When casserole is almost full, or you have used all the cabbage rolls, pour the remainder of tomato sauce over cabbage rolls. Bring casserole to a boil over medium heat. Place on a baking sheet in oven for 1 ½ to 2 hours or until cabbage rolls pierce easily with a fork. Add a little more tomato juice or water during baking if required. Remove from oven and serve hot. Cabbage rolls are best if they are refrigerated overnight and reheated before serving.

SERVES 6 TO 8.

City Chicken

It took me more than forty years to finally find this recipe. I was introduced as a child to City Chicken by my sister's Ukrainian mother-in-law. It was wonderful, even to my innocent taste buds. I didn't eat it again for years, but never forgot it. Forty years later a guest of Ukrainian descent, Vera Bochar, visited the Inn and gave me her recipe for "meat on a stick" or "Patichky." Although I remembered it as "City Chicken," you'll notice that the recipe doesn't contain a hint of chicken.

R

1 LB	VEAL	450 G
1 LB	PORK	450 G
1 LB	BEEF	450 G
1 TBSP	GARLIC, CHOPPED	15 ML
1 TBSP	FRESHLY GROUND PEPPER	15 ML
1 TBSP	PAPRIKA	15 ML
1 TSP	MARJORAM	5 ML
1 TSP	BASIL	5 ML
2 TSP	SALT	10 ML
1	LARGE ONION, COARSELY CHOPPED	1
1	EGG, BEATEN	1
1 TBSP	WATER	15 ML
	SALT AND PEPPER TO TASTE	
½ CUP	FLOUR	125 ML
2 CUPS	BREADCRUMBS	500 ML
¼ CUP	VEGETABLE OIL	50 ML
¼ CUP	BUTTER	50 ML
	WOODEN SKEWERS	

Cube veal, pork and beef into 1-inch / 2.5-cm chunks. Place in a glass bowl or casserole dish. Season with garlic, pepper, paprika, marjoram, basil and salt. Add coarsely chopped onion and toss. Cover and refrigerate overnight.

PREHEAT OVEN TO 300° F / 150° C.

Thread the meats tightly onto wooden skewers, alternating the three meats. Mix egg and water and season with salt and pepper. Dip skewered meat in flour and the egg mixture. Roll in breadcrumbs. Heat oil in a large frying pan over medium heat. Brown skewered meat lightly on all sides and layer in roasting pan. Dot with butter and bake, covered, for 1 to 1 ¼ hours or until tender.

SERVES 24.

1½ TO 2 LBS	BEEF TENDERLOIN	600 TO 900 G
1 TBSP	BUTTER	15 ML
1 TBSP	VEGETABLE OIL	15 ML
¼ CUP	BRANDY	50 ML
	BEEF BOUILLON FOR DEGLAZING FRYING PAN	
⅓ CUP	SOUR CREAM	75 ML
1 TSP	WORCESTERSHIRE SAUCE	5 ML
2 TSP	GREEN PEPPERCORNS	10 ML
¼ TSP	THYME	1 ML
	SALT TO TASTE	

Cut beef into steaks that are 1 inch / 2.5 cm thick. Melt butter and oil in a heavy frying pan over medium-high heat. Fry steaks, turning only once. Cook 3 to 4 minutes per side, for medium-rare. Pour brandy over steaks during last 30 seconds of cooking, and flame. Remove steaks to a hot platter; keep warm. Reduce heat; deglaze frying pan with a small amount of beef bouillon. Add sour cream and mix with brown bits in pan. Stir in Worcestershire sauce, peppercorns and thyme. Add salt to taste and serve over hot steaks.

SERVES 4.

GREEN PEPPERCORN STEAK

Gone are the days of the one-pound steak per person. Everyone is cutting back on red meat, but many of us don't want to completely eliminate it from our diets. We buy a whole tenderloin, which allows us to make servings the size we prefer. A good butcher will cut your steaks to order. The peppercorn sauce is a nice way to "dress up" a smaller portion.

W&R

TIP: *If you are counting calories, substitute low-fat yogurt for the sour cream.*

Hearty Beef Stew

Is anything so welcoming on a cold day as a hearty stew? Although we now use a pressure cooker, we used to begin preparing stew at noon so that it would be ready for supper. We were tied to the house for those six hours, but had the pleasure of the wonderful aroma and the anticipation. And what respectable stew would be seen in public without dumplings? Not this one! "Dough boys" are such an easy, economical addition.

W & R

1 ½ LBS	STEWING OR CHUCK BEEF	675 G
½ CUP	ALL-PURPOSE FLOUR	125 ML
½ TSP	GARLIC POWDER	2 ML
½ TSP	BASIL	2 ML
½ TSP	THYME	2 ML
½ TSP	PAPRIKA	2 ML
½ TSP	PEPPER	2 ML
½ TSP	SALT	2 ML
4 TBSP	VEGETABLE OIL	60 ML
2	ONIONS, QUARTERED	2
2	PARSNIPS	2
½	TURNIP	½
2	LARGE CARROTS	2
4	LARGE POTATOES, PEELED AND QUARTERED	4
1	BAY LEAF	1
¼ CUP	FRESH PARSLEY, CHOPPED	50 ML
2 CUPS	BEEF BOUILLON (OR RED WINE)	500 ML

Cut beef into 1 ½-inch / 4-cm cubes. Place flour and spices in a paper or plastic bag. Add cubed meat to the bag and gently shake until meat is well coated. Spray inside of pressure cooker with oil. Add oil to pressure cooker and place over medium-high heat. When pan is hot, add floured beef and brown on all sides turning occasionally, for about 10 minutes. When meat is browned, remove from pan and set aside. Heat more cooking oil, if necessary, and sauté onion until tender and light brown. Cut remaining

TIP: *A tasty stew depends on how well you've browned the meat, so don't try to rush the process. If you are using a large quantity of meat, brown it one layer at a time, placing the browned beef on a warm platter. Add a bit more oil on the pan and carefully brown the next layer.*

vegetables into chunks about the size of the beef. Add vegetable chunks, along with bay leaf, parsley, browned beef and bouillon or stock. Bring mixture to boil over high heat; put lid on cooker and attach pressure regulator. Reduce heat to medium. Cook until pressure regulator begins to rock.

PREPARE FLUFFY DUMPLINGS.

When regulator has rocked for 10 minutes, cool down pressure cooker by putting the pot under running cold water. Remove cooker lid, being careful of hot steam. Drop dumplings by the spoonful into the hot stew. Replace lid; cook on low heat 12 to 15 minutes. Open cooker and serve. Dumplings will be wonderfully fluffy and moist.

Serve with **Chow Chow** and **Flowering Crab-Apple Jelly**. An irrestible feast.

SERVES 4 TO 6.

Fluffy Dumplings

1 CUP	ALL-PURPOSE FLOUR	250 ML
1 TBSP	BAKING POWDER	15 ML
½ TSP	SALT	2 ML
3 TBSP	SHORTENING OR VEGETABLE OIL	45 ML
½ CUP	MILK	125 ML

Mix dry ingredients in a bowl. Blend in shortening or oil with fork or pastry blender. Add milk all at once; mix until well blended. Drop batter onto simmering stew.

Cover pot, simmer for 20 minutes in a conventional pot or 12 to 15 minutes in a pressure cooker.

MAKES 4 DUMPLINGS.

6	MEATY LAMB CHOPS	6
2 TBSP	OLIVE OIL	30 ML
1 TBSP	LEMON ZEST	15 ML
1 TBSP	BLACK PEPPER, FRESHLY GROUND	15 ML
1 TSP	DRIED THYME	5 ML
1 TSP	DRIED ROSEMARY, CRUMBLED	5 ML
¼ CUP	DRY BREADCRUMBS	50 ML

PREHEAT BROILER.

*M*oisten chops with olive oil, covering well. Combine lemon zest, pepper, thyme and rosemary with breadcrumbs in a small shallow pan or dish. Press chops into crumb mixture, coating well. Lightly oil a broiling pan or small baking pan; place chops about 3 inches / 7.5 cm under broiler. Watch carefully, turn when crumb mixture browns nicely and chops start to sizzle.

Remove from broiler when other side of chops brown and are sizzling. Serve on hot plates.

SERVES 3.

Lemon-Pepper Lamb Chops

Broiling requires added care and attention while cooking. If you have the time, the results are well worth the effort. Lamb chops love to spit and sputter under the broiler, so keep your eye on them to avoid burning. Be sure the fat is well trimmed but leave some on for excellent flavour. That being said, take pains to serve all lamb very hot as fat from cold lamb is not enjoyable.

W & R

Crusty Broiled Lamb Chops

Although we prefer fresh local lamb, we sometimes use the frozen, imported lamb for our own meals. We plan this meal a few days ahead so we can thaw the lamb in the refrigerator and let it sit for two or three days, a process which seems to tenderize the meat. The use of herbs enhances the flavour of lamb, so we use herbs and spices generously.

W&R

6 OR 8	LOIN LAMB CHOPS	6 OR 8
1 TBSP	VEGETABLE OIL	15 ML
1	CLOVE GARLIC, CHOPPED	1
	BLACK PEPPER, FRESHLY GROUND	
¼ CUP	BREADCRUMBS	50 ML
½ TSP	ROSEMARY, CRUSHED	2 ML
½ TSP	THYME	2 ML
½ TSP	BASIL	2 ML
1 TSP	LEMON RIND (ZEST), GRATED	5 ML
2 TBSP	GRAINY DIJON MUSTARD	30 ML

PREHEAT BROILER.

Choose fairly lean chops, or trim off excess fat. Coat chops in oil and finely chopped garlic. Sprinkle with lots of pepper; place under broiler for 3 to 4 minutes per side. Meanwhile, mix breadcrumbs with rosemary, thyme, basil and lemon zest. Remove chops from broiler. Butter top side with mustard. Divide seasoned breadcrumbs and press onto mustard-coated chops. Return to broiler for 4 to 5 minutes, watching carefully not to over-brown. Serve sizzling hot with **Mint Jelly**.

SERVES 2 TO 4.

4	CLOVES GARLIC	4
4 TO 5 LBS	LEG OF LAMB	2 TO 2.5 KG
2 Tbsp	OLIVE OIL	30 ML
2	BRANCHES FRESH ROSEMARY	2
2	BRANCHES FRESH THYME	2
½ TSP	BASIL	2 ML
	FRESHLY GROUND BLACK PEPPER	
	SALT	

PREHEAT OVEN TO 400° F / 200° C.

*P*eel garlic and slice into slivers. Using a sharp, small-bladed knife, cut slits in roast and insert garlic slivers. Drizzle oil over roast, rubbing well to cover. Pat chopped fresh rosemary and thyme onto oiled roast. Sprinkle with basil and black pepper. Place lamb in a small roasting pan; place in preheated oven. Reduce heat immediately to 325° F / 160° C. Roast uncovered for 1 ½ to 2 hours, until meat reaches 140° to 150° F / 60° to 65° C on thermometer, for medium-rare. Salt lightly before carving. Serve immediately on warm plates.

SERVES 6 TO 8.

*L*AMB *L*EG *R*OAST

Roast leg of lamb is an exquisite dish, and cooking it to perfection requires the use of a good meat thermometer. Use either the kind you insert and leave in the meat as it cooks or take readings with an instant registering thermometer to check the meat's progress. Don't over-cook lamb. It's at its very best when it's still pink, and served with homemade **Mint Jelly** or mint sauce.

W & R

Lamb Curry

There is nothing quite so delicious as a fine roasted leg of lamb, heavy with the flavours of fresh rosemary and garlic. And nothing else disappears so quickly, denying the creative cook the chance to work magic with leftovers. However, if you do have leftover lamb, this recipe will turn it into an East Indian feast.

W&R

2 TBSP	VEGETABLE OIL	30 ML
1	ONION, CHOPPED	1
2	CLOVES GARLIC, CHOPPED	2
1 TBSP	CURRY POWDER	15 ML
1 TSP	CUMIN POWDER	5 ML
1 TSP	FRESH GINGER ROOT, GRATED	5 ML
½ TSP	TURMERIC	2 ML
1 TBSP	WORCESTERSHIRE SAUCE	15 ML
1	STALK CELERY, CHOPPED	1
2	COOKING APPLES, CORED AND CHOPPED	2
1 OR 2 LBS	COOKED LAMB, CUT IN CUBES	450 TO 900 G
1 CUP	RAISINS OR CURRANTS	250 ML
1 CUP	BEEF OR CHICKEN BROTH	250 ML
	SALT AND PEPPER TO TASTE	
½ CUP	PLAIN YOGURT	125 ML
3 CUPS	COOKED WHITE RICE	750 ML
	CHUTNEY, PEANUTS, LARGE FLAKED COCONUT AND BOMBAY DUCK AS CONDIMENTS	

Heat oil in a large frying pan over medium heat; sauté onion and garlic for about 2 minutes, adding spices and stirring to release fragrances. The house should immediately start to smell wonderful! Add Worcestershire sauce, celery and apples; cook, stirring constantly, for about 5 minutes. Add lamb, raisins and broth. Cover and simmer for 5 minutes. Add salt and pepper to taste. Remove from heat and stir in yogurt. Serve immediately with rice. Pass a condiments tray containing one of our homemade chutneys, peanuts, large flaked coconut and Bombay duck (salted fish), if you have it on hand.

SERVES 4 TO 6.

Maple-Glazed Baked Ham Slices

2 LBS	HAM SLICES, FULLY COOKED AND BONELESS	1 KG
½ CUP	LIGHT BROWN SUGAR	125 ML
½ CUP	MAPLE SYRUP	125 ML
1 TBSP	PREPARED MUSTARD	15 ML

PREHEAT OVEN TO 350° F / 180° C.

Place ham on a greased, shallow roasting pan. Bake, covered with aluminum foil, for 15 minutes. Remove from oven. Mix the remaining ingredients in a small bowl.

To glaze: Turn oven temperature to 450° F / 230° C. Spread glaze over ham; bake for 10 minutes. Cut each slice in half. Serve with **Creamy Scalloped Potatoes** and **Hot Garlic Mustard** for a traditional Maritime dinner.

SERVES 4.

When the weather is cold, rainy and unfriendly, serve your family baked ham and potato scallop. Make enough so you can enjoy leftovers the next day. Then you can take a day off from cooking and curl up with a good book and a cup of cocoa. You may even be glad you're housebound!

W & R

129
MAIN DISHES
LAND & SEA

TIP: *Scalloped potatoes won't burn when reheated in a micro-wave oven.*

Maple-Apple Pork

This recipe is also good when prepared with chicken legs and thighs. Serve it with mashed potatoes or rice, or add some potatoes to the oven while it's baking. When the potatoes are done, cut a slit across the top, squeeze them open and drizzle with the maple sauce.

W&R

4 LBS	PORK TENDERLOIN	2 KG
1 TBSP	PAPRIKA	15 ML
1 TBSP	VEGETABLE OIL TO BROWN	15 ML
3	APPLES, PEELED AND SLICED	3
½ CUP	ONION, CHOPPED	125 ML
¼ CUP	DRY APPLE LIQUEUR OR APPLE JUICE CONCENTRATE	50 ML
½ CUP	CHICKEN STOCK	125 ML
1 TSP	THYME	5 ML
4 TBSP	MAPLE SYRUP	60 ML
	SALT AND PEPPER TO TASTE	
2 TBSP	BUTTER (OPTIONAL)	30 ML
1 TBSP	FLOUR (OPTIONAL)	15 ML

PREHEAT OVEN TO 375° F / 190° C.

Rinse tenderloins, pat dry and sprinkle with paprika. Heat oil in a cast iron frying pan and brown tenderloins over medium heat. Remove from pan and add apple and onion. Sauté until lightly browned. Add liqueur and chicken stock, stirring well while it bubbles. Return tenderloins to frying pan and sprinkle with thyme, spooning some of sauce mixture over meat. Cover and place in preheated oven for 30 minutes or until meat is tender and barely pink. Remove meat and slice it diagonally but not all the way through. Place on a heat-proof platter. Add maple syrup and salt and pepper to the frying pan sauce. Heat to boiling, stirring well. Thicken, if desired, using butter and flour. Pour hot sauce over sliced tenderloins and serve.

SERVES 6 TO 8.

1 LB	BONELESS PORK OR BONED CHICKEN BREASTS	450 G
3 TBSP	PEANUT BUTTER	45 ML
1 TBSP	RED WINE OR CIDER VINEGAR	15 ML
1 TBSP	SOY SAUCE	15 ML
1 TBSP	LIQUID HONEY	15 ML
1 TSP	GARLIC POWDER	5 ML
¼ TSP	SESAME OIL	1 ML
½ TSP	GINGER, POWDERED OR FRESHLY GRATED	2 ML
1 TSP	HOT PEPPER SAUCE	5 ML
½ TSP	SUGAR	2 ML

Sauté thinly sliced boneless pork or chicken in a small amount of oil in a non-stick pan until partially cooked. Add all other ingredients and stir well, while continuing to cook over a low heat. When meat is well coated with sauce, it is ready to serve.

This is delicious served with rice or fresh pasta and stir-fried vegetables.

SERVES 4.

SPICY PEANUTTY PORK
(OR CHICKEN)

Our son Greg was pretty skeptical when he saw me adding peanut butter to the pan of meat. However, he's always trusted my culinary decisions, so he didn't say too much. He really started talking once he'd sampled the recipe, and now he tells everyone about Spicy Peanutty Pork. It's one of his favourites.

R

Stuffed Pork Chops

Pork is a dish that always conjures up images for me of a special supper. Whenever we had pork, it seemed like a special occasion. Mum would often smother the chops in onions. But every now and then she would pull out all the stops and stuff thick, meaty chops with a savoury stuffing before letting them slowly brown and sizzle in a cast iron frying pan in the oven.

R

1 Tbsp	VEGETABLE OIL	15 ML
¼ CUP	ONION, FINELY CHOPPED	50 ML
⅛ CUP	CELERY, FINELY CHOPPED	25 ML
⅛ CUP	MUSHROOMS, CHOPPED	25 ML
½ CUP	COOKING APPLE, FINELY CHOPPED	125 ML
¼ TSP	MARJORAM	1 ML
½ TSP	SAVORY	2 ML
¼ TSP	THYME	1 ML
1½ CUPS	BREADCRUMBS	375 ML
	SALT AND PEPPER TO TASTE	
4	PORK CHOPS, 1½ INCHES / 3.5 CM THICK	4

PREHEAT OVEN TO 375° F / 190° C.

Heat oil in a cast iron frying pan over medium heat. Sauté onion and celery until soft; add mushrooms, apple and spices, continuing to cook for 2 to 3 minutes. When apple and mushrooms have mixed well with other ingredients, add breadcrumbs. (Mixture should be slightly moist. Add a small amount of water or apple juice, if required.) Add salt and pepper to taste. Remove from heat; cool.

To prepare pork chops, carefully cut slits in the side of each chop, allowing a pocket for the stuffing (or have your butcher do this for you). Place 2 Tbsp / 30 ml of stuffing into each chop. Secure opening with a toothpick. Brown chops over medium-high heat in the cast iron frying pan, and finish cooking by covering frying pan with foil and roasting in oven for 45 minutes. Serve hot.

SERVES 4.

Seasoned Breadcrumbs

2 CUPS	BREADCRUMBS	500 ML
3 TBSP	FRESH PARSLEY, CHOPPED	45 ML
½ CUP	PARMESAN CHEESE, GRATED	125 ML
¼ CUP	MOZZARELLA CHEESE, GRATED	50 ML
1 TBSP	GARLIC POWDER	15 ML
2 TSP	PAPRIKA	10 ML
¼ TSP	SALT	1 ML

Chicken

2	BONELESS CHICKEN BREASTS	2
½ CUP	FLOUR	125 ML
1	EGG (BEATEN WITH 1 TSP / 5 ML WATER)	1
1 TBSP	VEGETABLE OIL	15 ML
1 TBSP	FRESH LEMON JUICE	15 ML
1 TBSP	BUTTER OR MARGARINE	15 ML
	FRESH PARSLEY SPRIGS AND LEMON SLICES FOR GARNISHING	

Lover's Chicken

This is it, folks! The recipe that began the Mavis cooking team. Lover's Chicken was the basis of the very first dinner Ross cooked for us. It obviously worked, not that I'm one to tell tales out of the kitchen. It's now a favourite with our guests. Do try it. You'll love it.

W

Mix together all of the ingredients for the crumb mixture in a small cake pan and set aside.

Flatten chicken breasts to about ¼ inch / 5 mm by placing them between waxed paper and pounding firmly with a rolling pin. Peel flattened breast from paper and dredge in flour, then dip both sides of floured chicken in beaten egg. When well coated, place the floured chicken into crumb mixture. Cover thoroughly, pressing down firmly to coat chicken. Place crumbed breast back in waxed paper and reserve for cooking. Repeat until all breasts are coated.

Spray a large non-stick frying pan with vegetable spray. Add oil and place over medium heat. Sauté chicken cutlets 2 minutes on one side; turn and sauté other side until golden brown, 2 or 3 minutes. Place on a hot serving platter and return to stove. Add butter to the hot frying pan and squeeze in lemon juice. Deglaze pan by stirring quickly with a wooden spatula. Pour bubbling lemon butter sauce over chicken cutlets.

Garnish with sprigs of fresh parsley for colour. Serve with lemon slices and enjoy. I guarantee you'll be a lover of this chicken recipe.

SERVES 2.

Chicken Olivier

8	BONELESS CHICKEN BREASTS	8
	SALT AND PEPPER TO TASTE	
16	FRESH ASPARAGUS SPEARS	16
1 TBSP	GRATED LEMON ZEST	15 ML
¼ LB	SWISS CHEESE (CUT INTO 8 FINGERS)	125 G
12 OZ	LOBSTER MEAT	340 G
1 TBSP	VEGETABLE OIL	15 ML
½ CUP	ALL-PURPOSE FLOUR	125 ML
2	EGGS, BEATEN WITH A DASH OF SALT	2
3 CUPS	BREADCRUMBS	750 ML

PREHEAT OVEN TO 375° F / 190° C.

Carefully flatten chicken breasts into cutlets about ⅜ inch / 15 mm thick by placing them individually between sheets of plastic wrap and pounding gently with wooden mallet or rolling pin. Remove top sheet of plastic wrap and lightly sprinkle chicken with salt and pepper. Lay 2 asparagus spears end to end across the cutlet. Sprinkle about ¼ tsp / 1 ml of lemon zest on asparagus, lay cheese finger on asparagus and 2 or 3 Tbsp / 30 to 45 ml of lobster meat on top of cheese. Carefully roll plastic wrap so chicken wraps around contents to form a large sausage shaped roll. A small amount of asparagus should protrude from the ends. Refrigerate until firm. Heat oil in frying pan over medium heat. Remove chicken rolls from refrigerator and carefully unwrap them one at a time. Roll chicken in flour and in beaten egg and finally in the breadcrumbs. Brown two or three rolls at a time in hot pan, turning frequently, for 5 to 6 minutes. Remove browned chicken and place in lightly greased baking dish. Cover with foil and place in oven approximately 12 to 15 minutes until heated through and bubbling. Remove foil, slice rolls diagonally, and serve with cut interior sides exposed on plates. Elegant, beautiful and delicious.

SERVES 8.

Ross created this wonderful dish for Julie Kate Olivier, Sir Lawrence Olivier's daughter, who spent five weeks with us at the Inn. Julie Kate was in Saint John to play the part of Lady Macbeth in Shakespeare's *Macbeth* at the newly renovated Imperial Theatre. Director Tom Kerr, also staying at the Inn, arranged this special Valentine's supper for Julie Kate.

W & R

Chicken Pot Pie

We often purchase several chickens and freeze them for use in future recipes. Pot pie is one of our favourite meals. Sometimes, we make an extra pie to share with Ross's mother, who lives alone. Seniors tire of cooking. Many have been doing so for 60 or 70 years. If you have a senior family member or neighbour, surprise them with a pot pie and a bottle of home-made pickles. They'll really appreciate the gesture.

W

3 LBS	CHICKEN, WHOLE OR IN PIECES	1.5 KG
1	LARGE ONION, QUARTERED	1
1 TSP	SALT	5 ML
	FRESHLY GROUND BLACK PEPPER TO TASTE	
1	BAY LEAF	1
⅓ CUP	BUTTER	75 ML
1	CLOVE GARLIC	1
2 CUPS	UNCOOKED POTATOES, DICED	500 ML
3	LARGE CARROTS, PEELED, CUT INTO CHUNKS	3
2	LARGE ONIONS, QUARTERED	2
1 CUP	PEAS, FRESH OR FROZEN	250 ML
8	FRESH MUSHROOMS, QUARTERED	8
2 TBSP	ASSORTED HERBS, CHOPPED (PARSLEY, ROSEMARY AND/OR THYME)	30 ML
⅓ CUP	FLOUR	75 ML
3 CUPS	CHICKEN STOCK	750 ML
½ CUP	10% CREAM OR EVAPORATED MILK	125 ML
	SALT AND PEPPER TO TASTE	
	PASTRY DOUGH FOR 1 PIE SHELL	

*P*lace chicken, onion, salt, pepper and bay leaf in a large saucepan. Pour in enough water to cover chicken and bring to a boil, skimming off froth. Simmer, covered, for about 2 hours or until chicken is tender. Strain, reserving stock; discard onion and bay leaf. Cool chicken. Skin and bone; cut meat into large chunks and set aside.

Melt half of the butter in a saucepan over medium heat; sauté potatoes, carrots, onions, peas and mushrooms and assorted herbs for 5 minutes. Remove with a slotted spoon and set aside. Add remaining butter, stir in flour and cook, stirring constantly until bubbly. Mix in stock; cook, stirring until thickened and smooth. Add cream and heat through, but do not boil. Season sauce with salt and pepper.

PREHEAT OVEN TO 400° F / 200° C.

PREPARE AND CUT PASTRY.

Fold chicken and vegetables into sauce; spoon into an 8-cup / 2-litre shallow casserole, or 6 to 8 individual small casseroles. Cover with pastry. Brush with beaten egg. Bake on a baking sheet for 20 minutes or until pie is hot and bubbly and crust is lightly browned. (If crust browns too quickly, cover it with foil.)

    Chicken pot pie can be baked and eaten the same day. It is also possible to refrigerate the ingredients and assemble and bake the pie another day. The pot pie can also be completely assembled and frozen, then baked just as it is taken from the freezer.

SERVES 6 TO 8.

TIP: *To cut the pastry to fit your casserole, roll out dough, lay the top of the casserole over the pastry and cut around it. Make the top a little larger so you can press the extra dough along the outside of the dish. Decorate top with pastry leaves, held in place with an egg wash.*

Maple-Apple Chicken

Willa's mother and sister live in Gagetown, New Brunswick, so we regularly drive up the beautiful St. John River Valley. We particularly enjoy it in the fall, when the leaves on the hillsides are brilliant colours of red and yellow. We also like stopping at the several U-Pick apple farms and getting fresh, crisp apples for all our favourite recipes. This is one of them.

R

4	CHICKEN THIGHS WITH LEG ATTACHED	4
1 TBSP	PAPRIKA	15 ML
	VEGETABLE OIL FOR BROWNING	
2	APPLES, PEELED AND SLICED	2
½ CUP	ONION, CHOPPED	125 ML
½ CUP	CHICKEN STOCK OR APPLE JUICE	125 ML
1 TSP	THYME	5 ML
¼ CUP	MAPLE SYRUP	50 ML
	SALT AND PEPPER TO TASTE	
2 TBSP	BUTTER (OPTIONAL)	30 ML
1 TBSP	FLOUR (OPTIONAL)	15 ML

PREHEAT OVEN TO 375° F / 190° C.

Cut chicken thighs from legs. Rinse chicken pieces, pat dry and sprinkle with paprika. Heat oil in a cast iron frying pan and brown chicken over medium heat. Remove from pan; add apple and onion. Sauté until lightly browned. Stir in chicken stock or apple juice and keep stirring while it bubbles.

Return chicken pieces to frying pan, sprinkle with thyme and spoon sauce mixture over the meat. Cover and place in oven for 30 minutes until meat is tender and no longer pink near the bones. Remove meat and place on a platter.

Add maple syrup, salt and pepper to taste to the frying pan sauce. Heat until bubbling, stirring well. Thicken using butter and flour, if desired. Pour hot bubbling sauce over chicken and serve.

SERVES 4.

1 Tbsp	FRESH SAVORY, CHOPPED	15 ML	
1 Tbsp	FRESH MARJORAM, CHOPPED	15 ML	
¼ cup	HONEY	50 ML	
½ cup	ORANGE JUICE	125 ML	
2 tsp	LIGHT SOY SAUCE	10 ML	
8	CHICKEN DRUMSTICKS	8	
2 tsp	VEGETABLE OIL	10 ML	
2 tsp	CORNSTARCH	10 ML	
2 tsp	WATER	10 ML	

Savoury Honey-Glazed Chicken

This is a tasty recipe that can be made a day ahead, covered and stored in the refrigerator, or frozen for two months. Orange juice, savory, marjoram and honey make these drumsticks irresistible. You can build a meal around them, or use them as a nice "snackin' food." We take them with us when we attend country auctions. If you choose to follow our example, be sure to pack a few wet cloths 'cause they're finger lickin' good!

W & R

Combine herbs, honey, juice and soy sauce in a large bowl; add chicken and stir to coat. Cover and refrigerate 2 hours or overnight.

Preheat oven to 350° F / 180° C. Lightly oil an oven-proof pan and add chicken in a single layer, reserving marinade. Bake for 45 minutes, until chicken is tender, brushing occasionally with marinade, and rotating pieces to brown evenly. Remove chicken from dish. Set aside and keep warm.

Add remaining marinade to chicken dish. In a small separate bowl, blend cornstarch with water and stir into drippings. Place over medium-high heat for 3 minutes or until sauce boils and thickens slightly. Serve over chicken, accompanied by your favourite rice dish and fresh vegetables.

SERVES 4.

Savoury Crêpes

We like to make crêpes and eat them the same day, but we make enough to freeze for a quick meal later on, when we're rushed. We fill them with seafood, vegetables, cheese or leftover meat. They make a great main course or you can serve them as an appetizer.
W & R

3	EGGS, BEATEN	3
1½ CUPS	MILK	375 ML
1 TBSP	MELTED BUTTER OR VEGETABLE OIL	15 ML
1 CUP	ALL-PURPOSE FLOUR	250 ML
½ TSP	SALT	2 ML
	PINCH OF CAYENNE PEPPER	
2 TBSP	DILL, PARSLEY OR CHIVES, FINELY CHOPPED	50 ML

Place eggs, milk and butter in a blender or mixing bowl and blend or beat for about 30 seconds. Add flour, salt and cayenne and continue to beat for 2 to 3 minutes until mixture is the consistency of thick cream. Scrape down sides of bowl or blender and stir in chopped herbs. Place mixture in refrigerator for at least one hour or overnight.

Lightly oil a small non-stick frying pan. Place over medium heat and, when a drop of water dances on surface of pan, stir crêpe batter and add ¼ cup / 50 ml to pan. Tilt pan to coat surface evenly. Cook until golden brown on underside (usually 1 minute or less); turn and cook other side until lightly browned. Remove from heat and repeat process until all crêpes are cooked. Stack between sheets of waxed paper until needed.

These crêpes are excellent for seafood, poultry or meat fillings and can be used as an appetizer, luncheon dish or light entrée.

MAKES ABOUT 12 CRÊPES.

TURKEY-FILLED CRÊPES

¼ CUP	BUTTER OR VEGETABLE OIL	50 ML
¼ CUP	ALL-PURPOSE FLOUR	50 ML
1 ¾ CUPS	MILK	425 ML
	SALT AND PEPPER TO TASTE	
2 CUPS	COOKED TURKEY, CHOPPED	500 ML
1	CLOVE GARLIC, MINCED	1
½ TSP	WORCESTERSHIRE SAUCE	2 ML
1 CUP	BROCCOLI, COOKED AND CHOPPED	250 ML
⅛ CUP	RED PEPPER, CHOPPED	25 ML
	PARMESAN OR CHEDDAR CHEESE, GRATED	

PREPARE SAVOURY CRÊPES.

Melt butter or vegetable oil in a small saucepan or frying pan over medium heat. When it bubbles, add flour and mix well, letting mixture cook slightly for 20 to 30 seconds. Remove from heat and slowly add milk a little at a time, mixing well with wire whisk after each addition. Return to heat and stir for about 3 minutes until sauce thickens into a smooth, creamy consistency. Add salt and pepper to taste.

Add turkey, garlic, Worcestershire sauce and vegetables to sauce. Stir until well mixed and heated through. Taste and adjust for salt and pepper. Spoon about 2 heaping spoonsful of turkey mixture into each crêpe; roll up and place in a baking dish. Sprinkle rolled-up crêpes with cheese and place under broiler until cheese melts, watching carefully so that crêpes don't burn. Serve immediately with a side salad.

SERVES 6.

Turkey Croquettes

During the Christmas season, we were invited by CBC Radio to discuss uses for leftover turkey. This was one of the recipes we shared. We told the host we enjoy turkey leftovers so much we deliberately choose a turkey that's too big, or cook two at a time, so we will have lots of turkey for our favourite leftover recipes. His look seemed to say, "It takes all kinds."

W & R

2 CUPS	COOKED TURKEY MEAT, COARSELY CHOPPED	500 ML
1 TBSP	ONION, CHOPPED	15 ML
1 TBSP	FRESH PARSLEY, CHOPPED	15 ML
1 TSP	WORCESTERSHIRE SAUCE	5 ML
½ TSP	HOT PEPPER FLAKES	2 ML
¼ TSP	CURRY POWDER	1 ML
¼ TSP	THYME	1 ML
⅔ CUP	GRAVY OR 18% CREAM	150 ML
1	EGG YOLK	1
½ CUP	MILK OR 10% CREAM	125 ML
2	SLICES COOKED HAM, THICKLY CUT	2
	FLOUR FOR DREDGING	
	SEASONED BREADCRUMBS	

Process turkey meat in a food processor until pieces are the size of large breadcrumbs. Add chopped onion and parsley and process a few more seconds until well blended. Place in a bowl and mix with Worcestershire sauce, pepper flakes, curry powder and thyme.

Heat gravy in a frying pan over medium heat until it's bubbling. Add egg yolk and remove pan from burner, mixing well. Cool. Add turkey mixture and blend thoroughly. Chill in refrigerator at least 1 hour to produce a firm mixture.

PREPARE SEASONED BREADCRUMBS.

Cut ham into pencil-sized sticks about 2 inches / 5 cm long. Shape turkey mixture around ham stick. Roll into shape of sausage or drumstick. Dredge in flour; dip in milk, then coat with crumb mixture. Let dry about 10 minutes. Sauté in hot oil in a frying pan until golden brown and crisp. Serve hot.

SERVES 4.

¼ CUP	LEMON JUICE	50 ML
¼ CUP	VEGETABLE OR OLIVE OIL	50 ML
½ CUP	TURKEY OR CHICKEN BROTH	125 ML
½ CUP	FRESH PARSLEY, CHOPPED	125 ML
2	GREEN ONIONS, FINELY CHOPPED	2
1 TO 2 TBSP	DIJON MUSTARD	15 TO 30 ML
1 TBSP	TARRAGON (OR 1 TSP/5 ML CURRY POWDER)	15 ML
3 ½ CUPS	COOKED PASTA (MACARONI, PENNE, SHELLS OR FUSILLI)	875 ML
3 ½ CUPS	COOKED TURKEY, CHOPPED	875 ML
½ CUP	CELERY, CHOPPED	125 ML
½ CUP	RED AND GREEN PEPPERS, CHOPPED	125 ML
	SALT AND PEPPER TO TASTE	

TURKEY SALAD

What do you with turkey left-overs? We all look forward to the hot turkey dinner and enjoy the first sandwich, but then what? We've developed several uses for our leftover turkey; this salad is one of our favourites because it's so completely different from the original dinner.

W&R

Whisk lemon juice in a mixing bowl while adding oil in a steady stream. Continue whisking and gradually add broth, parsley, green onions, Dijon mustard and tarragon. (For a completely different taste, omit tarragon and add curry powder.) Add cooked pasta, turkey, celery and peppers to dressing. Add salt and pepper to taste and mix well. Cover and refrigerate for 30 minutes to an hour before serving.

SERVES 4 TO 6.

143
MAIN DISHES
LAND & SEA

Turkey-Stuffed Peppers

This is a great use for leftover turkey and ham. It makes a nice, light lunch and all the ingredients can be prepared ahead of time so you aren't in the kitchen, slaving over a hot stove, while your guests are having a good time in the living room. When your guests arrive, pop the peppers in the oven. Sit down with a glass of sherry, join in the conversation and wait for the timer to ring. How civilized!

W & R

1	SMALL ONION, CHOPPED	1
2 TBSP	VEGETABLE OIL	30 ML
1 CUP	WHITE AND/OR WILD RICE, COOKED	250 ML
1 TSP	THYME	5 ML
½ TSP	MARJORAM	2 ML
1 CUP	COOKED TURKEY, CHOPPED	250 ML
½ CUP	COOKED HAM, CHOPPED	125 ML
	SALT AND PEPPER TO TASTE	
1 CUP	TURKEY GRAVY OR CONSOMMÉ	250 ML
	DASH OF SHERRY	
¼ CUP	10% CREAM	50 ML
4	SWEET PEPPERS (RED, GREEN OR YELLOW)	4

PREHEAT OVEN TO 375° F / 190° C.

Sauté onion in oil in a small frying pan. Add rice, thyme and marjoram; stir well. Mix in chopped turkey and ham. Add salt and pepper to taste. Remove from heat; place in bowl to cool.

Add gravy or consommé to same frying pan over medium heat. Bring mixture to a boil and stir in sherry. Reduce temperature slightly and add cream. Mix well; remove from heat. Set aside.

Cut stems off peppers. Cut off tops, removing seeds and cores. Fill peppers with turkey-rice mixture. Spoon sherry gravy into filled peppers. Place peppers in a lightly oiled small baking dish. Cover with foil. Bake for about 20 minutes until hot and peppers are soft. Serve at once.

SERVES 4.

JAMBALAYA

4	PORK SAUSAGES	4
2 TBSP	OLIVE OIL	30 ML
1	ONION, FINELY CHOPPED	1
2	CLOVES GARLIC, FINELY CHOPPED	2
1	GREEN PEPPER, FINELY CHOPPED	1
½ LB	COOKED HAM, COARSELY DICED	225 G
½ LB	COOKED CHICKEN	225 G
1 LB	JUMBO SHRIMP, SHELLED	450 G
½ CUP	DRY WHITE WINE	125 ML
19-OZ CAN	ITALIAN TOMATOES	540-ML CAN
1 CUP	LONG-GRAIN RICE, UNCOOKED	250 ML
2 TBSP	FRESH PARSLEY, CHOPPED	30 ML
1	BAY LEAF	1
¼ TSP	OREGANO	1 ML
¼ TSP	THYME	1 ML
1 TSP	TABASCO SAUCE	5 ML
	SALT AND CAYENNE PEPPER TO TASTE	

Jambalaya is probably the most famous dish from Louisiana. Red Jambalaya is Creole while the brown variety is Cajun. Maritimers have strong links with Louisiana. The Cajun people trace their heritage directly to our Acadian families, and both groups play an important part in their region's cuisine. So, to our cousins to the south, thanks for sharing this exciting dish.

W&R

Cut sausages into 1-inch / 2.5-cm chunks. Fry in a heavy casserole over medium heat until lightly browned; remove and set aside. Add olive oil, onion and garlic to casserole; sauté until onion is soft. Mix in green pepper, ham, chicken and shrimp. Stir well and sauté for 1 minute. Add wine and tomatoes (liquid should total 2 cups) as well as rice, seasonings and sausages. Stir well and cover. Reduce heat and simmer for 20 to 25 minutes. Serve when rice is fully cooked and tender.

SERVES 6.

Fettucine Marinara

Fresh herbs are available all year round. Fresh fish and seafood are flown from both coasts to central Canada on a daily basis. When we were living in Toronto, we had a longing for fresh haddock. We went to St. Lawrence Market and found some that had just been flown in from Saint John! It was like being home. Try to find fresh herbs and seafood for this recipe; your taste-buds will be rewarded.

W & R

¼ CUP	OLIVE OIL	50 ML
1	ONION, CHOPPED	1
1	CLOVE GARLIC, CRUSHED	1
1 LB	FRESH TOMATOES, CHOPPED	450 ML
¼ CUP	DRY WHITE WINE	50 ML
2 TSP	BROWN SUGAR	10 ML
1 TBSP	FRESH OREGANO, CHOPPED	15 ML
1 TBSP	FRESH BASIL, CHOPPED	15 ML
1½ LBS	FRESH SEAFOOD, (SHRIMP, SCALLOPS, MUSSELS AND/OR SQUID)	675 G
½ LB	FRESH PASTA	225 G
1	LEMON, CUT IN WEDGES	1
	PARMESAN CHEESE, GRATED	
	FRESHLY GROUND BLACK PEPPER	

Heat oil in a large frying pan over medium heat; add onion and garlic and sauté for 2 minutes or until onion is soft. Stir in chopped tomatoes, wine, sugar and herbs. Bring to a boil; reduce heat, then cover and simmer for 15 minutes until sauce thickens slightly. Stir in your choice of uncooked seafood; simmer for 5 minutes or until seafood is cooked but still tender.

Cook pasta according to directions on the package; drain. Place pasta in a large serving bowl or individual bowls. Top with seafood sauce. Garnish with lemon wedges and season with Parmesan cheese and freshly ground pepper.

SERVES 4.

2 CUPS	WATER	500 ML
1 LB	HADDOCK	450 G
½ LB	SCALLOPS	225 G
¼ LB	SHRIMP, SHELLED	115 G
2 TBSP	CHICKEN BOUILLON CONCENTRATE	30 ML
2 TBSP	BUTTER	30 ML
6 TBSP	ALL-PURPOSE FLOUR	90 ML
1 CUP	CHEDDAR CHEESE, GRATED	250 ML
2	EGG YOLKS	2
1 CUP	10% CREAM OR EVAPORATED MILK	250 ML
1 TBSP	BUTTER OR MARGARINE	15 ML
1 CUP	MUSHROOMS	250 ML
½ TSP	WORCESTERSHIRE SAUCE	2 ML
10 OZ	LOBSTER MEAT	300 G
1 TBSP	DULSE FLAKES	15 ML
	CAYENNE PEPPER TO TASTE	
	SALT TO TASTE	
¼ CUP	FRESHLY CHOPPED PARSLEY	50 ML
	BUTTERED BREAD CUBES OR CROUTONS FOR TOPPING	

This is our traditional Christmas Eve dinner. With all the turkey, ham and lamb we consume over the twelve days of the holiday season, seafood dinner is a welcome treat.

W&R

PREHEAT OVEN TO 425° F / 220° C.

Bring water to a boil in a large saucepan; add fresh haddock, scallops and shrimp. Simmer about 4 minutes. Remove fish and seafood using a slotted spoon and set aside. Transfer liquid to a large bowl and add chicken bouillon to make 2 cups. Melt butter in the saucepan over medium heat; stir in flour and cook briefly. Gradually beat in hot reserved liquid. Cook, stirring well. As sauce thickens, blend in cheese. Remove from heat.

In a separate bowl, mix egg yolks with cream; beat briefly and add to sauce. Beat well until blended and smooth. Melt butter in a small frying pan and sauté mushrooms. Add to sauce with Worcestershire sauce, seafood (including lobster) and dulse flakes. Stir well; add cayenne pepper and salt; sprinkle with parsley. Pour into a 12-cup / 3-litre oiled casserole and cover with buttered breadcrumbs or croutons. Bake 15 minutes, until hot and bubbly. Serve with steamed rice or pasta.

SERVES 6 TO 8.

GINGER SHRIMP IN PASTRY

1 LB	FRESH SHRIMP (ABOUT 26 TO 30), SHELLED	450 G
2 TBSP	VEGETABLE OIL	30 ML
1 TBSP	FLOUR	15 ML
1 TSP	FRESH GINGER ROOT, GRATED	5 ML
1 TSP	GARLIC, CHOPPED	5 ML
½ TSP	CHILI PEPPER FLAKES	2 ML
1 TBSP	HONEY	15 ML
½ CUP	DRY WHITE WINE	125 ML
½ CUP	CEREAL CREAM	125 ML
2	GREEN ONIONS, CHOPPED	2
	SALT TO TASTE	
	PUFF PASTRY FOR CRUST	
1	EGG, BEATEN	1

PREHEAT OVEN TO 400° F / 200° C.

Rinse and dry shrimp; set aside. Heat oil in a large non-stick frying pan over medium heat; stir in flour and ginger root. Add garlic, pepper flakes and honey. While bubbling, mix in white wine. Add shrimp; stir well to coat with bubbling sauce. Cook for 2 minutes, turning shrimp once. Quickly stir in cream and mix well until thickened, being careful not to boil after cream has been added. Stir in onions and add salt to taste.

Place mixture in serving-sized oven-proof dishes. Brush beaten egg on rim of dishes to allow pastry to seal around edges. Roll out puff pastry until ¼ inch / 5mm thick and cover each dish, folding pastry slightly over edge of ramekin. Decorate top of pastry with pastry flowers. Brush pastry tops with remaining beaten egg and bake 10 minutes, or until pastry is puffed and golden brown. Serve with salad or coleslaw and hot crusty rolls.

SERVES 4.

My working life has taken me across Canada, and in my moves from West to East I've observed some changes that occur in the English language. Small shrimp on the West Coast are called shrimp, the larger ones prawns. Here they're all called shrimp. The main thing to remember is that no matter what you call them, shrimp are a wonderful seafood delicacy. Try this recipe and you won't call them shrimp or prawns, you'll call them fantastic!

R

Jumbo Shrimp Linguine

When we were kids, pasta meant macaroni. Now the choices of dried and fresh pasta seem endless. We've even made our own, but we must admit that buying it fresh from our local pasta maker makes more sense. He has several varieties, all made without egg or oil, so they are good and healthy. Next to his shop is the fish market and the vegetable stall, so after three stops, we're well on our way to a great dinner.

W & R

2 TBSP	VEGETABLE OIL	30 ML
1	CLOVE GARLIC, MINCED	1
¼ CUP	GREEN ONION, FINELY CHOPPED	50 ML
¼ CUP	RED PEPPER, CHOPPED	50 ML
½ LB	MUSHROOMS, SLICED	225 G
2 TSP	FRESH DILL, CHOPPED	10 ML
2 TBSP	FRESH PARSLEY, CHOPPED	30 ML
1 LB	JUMBO SHRIMP, COOKED	450 G
1 CUP	LOW-FAT SOUR CREAM OR YOGURT	250 ML
1 LB	FRESH LINGUINE	450 G
2 TBSP	BUTTER OR MARGARINE	30 ML
½ CUP	PARMESAN CHEESE, FRESHLY GRATED	125 ML
	FRESHLY GROUND BLACK PEPPER TO TASTE	
	FRESH DILL OR PARSLEY AND LEMON WEDGES FOR GARNISHING	

Heat half the oil in a frying pan and gently sauté garlic, onion and red pepper. Remove and set aside. Heat remaining oil and sauté mushrooms until lightly browned. Return onion mixture to the pan over low heat; add dill, parsley and cooked shrimp. Stir in sour cream and keep warm.

Cook linguine according to directions on package. Toss with butter and half the Parmesan cheese.

Arrange noodles on a warm platter or on individual plates; ladle seafood sauce over them. Sprinkle with extra Parmesan and freshly ground pepper. Garnish with fresh dill or parsley and lemon wedges.

SERVES 4.

CRUST

¼ LB	BUTTER OR MARGARINE, SOFTENED	115G
1 CUP	FLOUR	250 ML
¼ TSP	SALT	1 ML

FILLING

1¾ CUPS	MOZZARELLA CHEESE, GRATED	425 ML
1	SMALL ONION, SLICED AND SAUTÉED	1
¼ LB	MUSHROOMS, SLICED AND SAUTÉED	115 G
8 OZ	LOBSTER MEAT	225 G
	JUICE OF ONE LEMON	
4	EGGS	4
1½ CUPS	MILK OR 10% CREAM	375 ML
¼ TSP	SALT	1 ML
⅛ TSP	PEPPER	.5 ML
⅛ TSP	NUTMEG	.5 ML
	LEMON WEDGES FOR GARNISHING	

LOBSTER QUICHE

Remember when "real men" didn't eat quiche? They started eating it again when they tasted this one!

W & R

PREHEAT OVEN TO 375° F / 190° C.

Cut margarine into flour and salt and mix until a ball forms. Pat dough with hands into a 9-inch / 23-cm pie plate or your favourite quiche pan. That's it! Simple and foolproof.

To prepare filling, mix together grated cheese, onion, mushrooms and lobster and put into pie shell. Squeeze lemon juice over mixture. Lightly beat eggs and milk in a large bowl. Add salt, pepper and nutmeg; pour into pie shell. Bake 35 to 40 minutes or until a knife inserted in centre comes out clean. Allow to stand 10 minutes before cutting. Garnish with lemon wedges and serve with coleslaw and rolls or biscuits.

SERVES 4 TO 6.

TIP: *Quiche is best served just above room temperature rather than hot from the oven.*

_L_obster _R_olls

When my dear mother visited us in Toronto, she was 84 years old and rather feeble. Still up for a good time, however, she agreed to go out for several meals. I really wanted her to experience the unique restaurants along Bloor Street. The day we headed out she announced she wasn't too hungry and said, "I think I'll just have a Lobster Roll." I laughed and explained to her that we weren't in the Maritimes. This everyday lunch in Saint John was not to be found in Canada's largest city. No wonder we moved back!

_W & R_

1 CUP	LOBSTER MEAT	250 ML
½ CUP	CELERY, FINELY DICED	125 ML
3 TBSP	MAYONNAISE	45 ML
1 TSP	LEMON JUICE	5 ML
2	HOT DOG ROLLS, BUTTERED AND TOASTED	2
2 TBSP	LETTUCE, FINELY SLICED	30 ML

_D_rain and coarsely chop lobster meat, removing cartilage or any shell pieces. Combine lobster, celery, salad dressing and lemon juice in a small bowl. Spoon into warm hot dog rolls lined with lettuce. Serve immediately.

SERVES 2.

CRAB & LOBSTER CRÊPES

12	CRÊPES	12
1 CUP	SOUR CREAM	250 ML
2 TBSP	FRESH CHIVES, CHOPPED	30 ML
1 TBSP	LEMON JUICE	15 ML
¼ CUP	SWISS CHEESE, GRATED	50 ML
½ TSP	FRESHLY GROUND BLACK PEPPER	2 ML
	SALT TO TASTE	
2 6.5-OZ CANS	CRAB MEAT, DRAINED AND FLAKED	2 368-G CANS
10 OZ	LOBSTER MEAT, COOKED AND DRAINED	300 G
½ CUP	BREADCRUMBS	125 ML
¼ CUP	PARMESAN CHEESE, GRATED	50 ML
¼ CUP	MELTED BUTTER	50 ML
	LEMON WEDGES FOR GARNISHING	

Crab and lobster are both fished in the Maritimes, so we can generally buy them at the same time in our stores. This recipe makes a wonderful lunch, and most of the preparation can be done well in advance. Cold Clamato juice adorned with a celery stick and a small tossed salad or coleslaw will be all you need to satisfy the most discerning tastes.

W & R

PREHEAT OVEN TO 350° F / 180° C.

PREPARE SAVOURY CRÊPES.

Combine sour cream, chives, lemon juice, cheese and pepper in a large mixing bowl. Check crab meat for pieces of shell; thaw and drain lobster, cutting larger pieces into bite-sized chunks. Blend with sour cream mixture, stirring well. Taste and adjust seasoning for salt. Spoon ¼ cup / 50 ml of mix onto centre of each crêpe. Roll up and place in an oiled 13 x 9 x 2-inch / 3.5-litre baking dish. Sprinkle with breadcrumbs and Parmesan cheese and drizzle with butter. Bake for 20 minutes or until hot and bubbly. Garnish with fresh lemon wedges.

SERVES 6 FOR LUNCH.

CRAB CAKES

I've sailed the Chesapeake. And I've eaten famous crab cakes in Annapolis, Chesapeake City, and at the Harbourfront in Baltimore. Sorry, Maryland, these are better.

8 OZ	CRAB MEAT, COOKED AND DRAINED	225 G
¾ CUP	BREADCRUMBS	175 ML
1	EGG YOLK	1
1 TSP	DRY MUSTARD	5 ML
2 TSP	WORCESTERSHIRE SAUCE	10 ML
1 TBSP	MAYONNAISE	15 ML
2 TSP	FRESH PARSLEY, CHOPPED	10 ML
1 TSP	LEMON JUICE	5 ML
½ TSP	GARLIC, CHOPPED	2 ML
1	GREEN ONION, CHOPPED	1
½ TBSP	PAPRIKA	7 ML
1 TBSP	BUTTER, MELTED	15 ML
1 TBSP	VEGETABLE OIL	15 ML
	LEMON WEDGES FOR GARNISHING	

Carefully pick through crab meat, removing and discarding pieces of shell. Place crab in a large bowl and mix with breadcrumbs. In a separate bowl, combine egg, dry mustard, Worcestershire sauce, mayonnaise, parsley, lemon juice, garlic, onion, paprika and butter. Mix thoroughly with crab. Shape into 6 cakes. Cool in refrigerator at least 30 minutes. Heat oil in a large frying pan over medium heat, add crab cakes and fry, turning once, until golden brown (about 3 minutes per side). Garnish with lemon wedges. These cakes are also delicious with homemade **Cucumber Sauce.**

MAKES 6 CAKES. SERVES 2 TO 3.

1 CUP	FLOUR	250 ML
1½ TSP	BAKING POWDER	7 ML
¼ TSP	SALT	1 ML
¼ TSP	PEPPER	1 ML
¼ TSP	PAPRIKA	1 ML
1 TBSP	FRESH PARSLEY, CHOPPED	15 ML
1	SMALL ONION, FINELY CHOPPED	1
1	EGG, SEPARATED	1
½ CUP	MILK	125 ML
2 CUPS	STEAMED CLAMS, SHELLED AND MINCED	500 ML

Mix dry ingredients in a bowl. Stir in parsley and onion. Separate egg into two bowls. Beat yolk with milk and add to dry ingredients. Mix well. Stiffly beat egg whites and fold into mixture. Add clams and stir gently. Heat oil in a frying pan over medium heat and drop in spoonfuls of clam mixture. Fry one side until edges begin to brown and fritter starts to dry. Turn over and cook other side until brown and crisp, about 5 minutes. These fritters are delicious with homemade **Cucumber Sauce**.

Makes 12 4-inch / 10-cm fritters.

SERVES 4.

Clam Fritters

When I was very young, a trip to dig clams was like a journey to a different world. Somehow, Dad knew when the tide would be low, and as soon as we arrived, we'd begin digging, carefully coached on where to find these elusive bivalves. When we arrived home with our full buckets, Mum would get the huge kettle boiling and we would sit down to a feast of homemade rolls and clams dipped in melted butter. There were always leftover clams, and they were turned into fritters the next day.

W

155
MAIN DISHES
LAND & SEA

Cucumber Sauce

This delicate sauce is especially good with **Clam Fritters** and the **Crab Cakes**. But be sure to try it on something as simple as pan-fried haddock. It's a nice alternative to tartar sauce, which many people find can upset their tummies.

W & R

1 CUP	CUCUMBER, PEELED, SEEDED AND CHOPPED	250 ML
½ CUP	WATER	125 ML
2 TBSP	BUTTER	30 ML
2 TBSP	FLOUR	30 ML
1 TBSP	LEMON JUICE	15 ML
½ TSP	GARLIC, CHOPPED	2 ML
1	LEMON RIND (ZEST), GRATED	1
½ TSP	SALT	2 ML
	PEPPER TO TASTE	
1 TSP	DILL	5 ML
1 TBSP	CAPERS	15 ML

Cook cucumber in water until tender. Drain and reserve cucumber and cooking liquid. Add enough water to this liquid to make 1 cup / 250 ml. Melt butter in a small saucepan and blend in flour. Add reserved liquid slowly and mix well until thickened.

Stir in lemon juice, garlic, zest, salt, pepper, dill, capers and cucumber. Mix well. Taste and adjust spices. Serve warm over fish.

MAKES 1½ CUPS / 375 ML.

¼ CUP	VEGETABLE OIL	50 ML
1	SMALL ONION, CHOPPED	1
4	CLOVES GARLIC, CHOPPED	4
⅓ CUP	FRESH PARSLEY, CHOPPED	75 ML
2	BAY LEAVES	2
½ TSP	THYME	2 ML
½ TSP	OREGANO	2 ML
½ TSP	ROSEMARY	2 ML
2 CUPS	DRY WHITE WINE	500 ML
3 LBS	FRESH CULTIVATED MUSSELS	1.5 KG

Heat oil in a large frying pan over medium heat and sauté onion until soft. Stir in chopped garlic, parsley, bay leaves and other herbs.

Pour in wine and bring to a boil. Add live mussels, cover with lid and bring back to the boil. Steam until mussels open, about 4 minutes. Remove mussels from pan with a slotted spoon. Pour hot herbed broth over mussels and serve with crusty bread.

SERVES 4.

Herbed Mussels

Archaeologists tell us this mollitreusk has been used as food for over 20,000 years. It is only recently that mussels have become popular in North America, although prior to the arrival of European settlers, native North Americans prized them as food and for their decorative shells. Cultivated mussels from New Brunswick and Prince Edward Island are a real treat, and they are available throughout the year. Like other shellfish, mussels should be fresh and alive for cooking.

W & R

Seafood & Spinach Crêpes

This seafood and spinach crêpe combines the robust flavour of smoked salmon with the delicate creaminess of Coquille St-Jacques and the spring garden flavour of spinach. It is a union that is truly blessed!

W & R

12	CRÊPES	12
¾ LB	FRESH SCALLOPS	350 G
1 TBSP	BUTTER	15 ML
1 TBSP	ONION, FINELY CHOPPED	15 ML
¼ CUP	DRY VERMOUTH OR WHITE WINE	50 ML
1¼ CUPS	10% CREAM	300 ML
1	EGG YOLK, BEATEN	1
¼ CUP	SMOKED SALMON, CHOPPED	50 ML
1½ CUPS	FRESH SPINACH, COOKED AND CHOPPED, OR FROZEN SPINACH, THAWED, SQUEEZED DRY AND CHOPPED	400 ML
	SALT AND PEPPER TO TASTE	
	PARMESAN CHEESE, GRATED	
	FRESH PARSLEY FOR GARNISHING	

PREHEAT OVEN TO 375° F / 180° C.

PREPARE SAVORY CRÊPES.

Wash scallops briefly in cold water and pat dry. If scallops are bigger than a walnut, cut them in two. Melt butter in a saucepan over medium-high heat; add scallops and chopped onion. Sauté until onion is soft and scallops are slightly opaque, about 3 minutes, shaking pan frequently to avoid burning. Pour in vermouth or wine and simmer 2 minutes. Add cream and beaten egg yolk, stirring frequently; simmer for an additional 5 minutes to thicken sauce slightly. Combine smoked salmon and spinach; blend into mixture. Add salt and pepper to taste. Remove saucepan from heat. Place a heaping tablespoon of the mixture in centre of each crêpe and roll up. Place rolled crêpes in a shallow, heat-proof 12-cup / 3-litre dish; sprinkle with Parmesan cheese and pour remaining sauce over crêpes. Place in oven for 5 minutes until crêpes are warm. Serve with parsley as a garnish.

SERVES 6.

6	LARGE POTATOES, PEELED	6
¼ CUP	BUTTER	50 ML
½ TSP	FRESHLY GROUND BLACK PEPPER	2 ML
1 LB	SALT COD	450 G
1	ONION, FINELY CHOPPED	1
2	EGGS	2
1 TSP	DULSE FLAKES OR NORI FLAKES	5 ML
	CORNMEAL	
	VEGETABLE OIL FOR FRYING	

*B*oil potatoes without salt in a large saucepan over medium heat until cooked. Drain, mashing well with butter and pepper. Rinse salt cod lightly with cold water. Put fish into a separate saucepan and cover with hot water. Boil gently 10 to 15 minutes until softened. Drain and flake salt cod, and add to potatoes. Heat a small amount of butter in a small frying pan and sauté onion until soft; add to mashed potato mixture along with eggs and dulse flakes and mix well.

Cool mixture until firm and form into cakes. Pat cakes in cornmeal to coat, covering them well. Refrigerate until ready to eat. To cook, heat a small amount of oil in a large frying pan and fry fishcakes over medium heat, about 5 minutes on each side, until golden brown and crispy.

To prepare as my Mum did for Dad and the family: Cook 1 piece of bacon per person in a heavy frying pan. Remove bacon and keep warm on the back of the stove. In the same pan, fry fishcakes in a small amount of bacon fat until brown on one side: Turn and cook other side until golden brown, about 5 minutes per side. Serve hot and crispy with a fried egg and bacon on the side, along with **Mustard Pickles** or **Chow Chow**.

MAKES ABOUT 2 DOZEN CAKES. SERVES 4 TO 6.

Down East Codfish Cakes

When my parents had a fish stall in our local market, Mum made fish cakes several nights a week to sell the next day. She continued making them well into her 80s. Patting the warm, soft mixture between her weathered hands, she would say, "If I had a nickel for every fish cake I ever made . . ." and her voice would trail off, as I suppose she did some rough math in her mind. Ross and I use her recipe, varying it only by adding onion and dulse flakes. Made either Mum's way or ours, you'll love them!

W

Haddock in Phyllo Pastry

Haddock is the most popular white fish in the Maritimes. It's readily available fresh or frozen. Fresh haddock is preferred in most recipes, like this one, but keep a package of frozen haddock in your freezer: it's great in any of the chowder recipes. This recipe takes a little longer to cook because the pastry acts like insulation.

W & R

TIP: *There are two rules when cooking fresh fish: buy it as fresh as you can, and cook it as little as you can, no more than 10 minutes per inch / 2.5 cm.*

8 OZ	FRESH SPINACH	200 G
1½ LBS	HADDOCK FILLETS	675 G
4 TBSP	GRAINY DIJON MUSTARD	60 ML
½ CUP	PARMESAN CHEESE	125 ML
	FRESHLY GROUND BLACK PEPPER	
8	SHEETS PHYLLO PASTRY	8
½ CUP	BUTTER, MELTED	125 ML

PREHEAT OVEN TO 400° F / 200° C.

Remove large stems from the largest spinach leaves (large enough to wrap fish). Place leaves in a steamer and blanch for 2 to 3 minutes or until leaves are limp.

Using your fingers and a pair of tweezers, remove bones from haddock fillets. Cut into 4 pieces.

Place enough spinach leaves on waxed paper to wrap one fillet. Place haddock on spinach. Spread half the mustard on top of fish. Sprinkle with Parmesan cheese and pepper. Fold spinach over fillet and wrap in waxed paper. Repeat for each fillet.

Carefully baste one phyllo sheet with melted butter; top with other sheet, basting with butter as well. Carefully remove spinach-wrapped haddock fillet from waxed paper and gently place on pastry sheets. Wrap pastry around fish, closing off ends. Brush melted butter on phyllo packet and place on baking sheet. Bake for 15 to 20 minutes until pastry packets are golden brown.

SERVES 4.

FISHERMAN'S STEW

2 TBSP	BUTTER OR VEGETABLE OIL	30 ML
1	LARGE ONION, SLICED PAPER THIN	1
1 TBSP	FLOUR	15 ML
19-OZ CAN	TOMATOES, UNDRAINED	540-ML CAN
2 TSP	SALT	10 ML
½ TSP	PEPPER	2 ML
¼ CUP	FRESH PARSLEY, CHOPPED	50 ML
½ TSP	SAVORY	2 ML
¼ TSP	DRY MUSTARD	1 ML
¼ TSP	GINGER	1 ML
1 LB	HADDOCK FILLETS, FRESH OR FROZEN	450 G
2	EGGS	2
2 TBSP	LEMON JUICE	30 ML
2 TBSP	BUTTER (OPTIONAL)	30 ML

We call fish "fast food." A salmon or haddock fillet can be baked in 10 minutes, barely giving you time to prepare the vegetables. This is another example of a fast fish dinner, with the added bonus of being prepared in one pot. We've made it quickly when family have dropped in unexpectedly. If you have a pound of haddock in the freezer and a can of tomatoes in the cupboard, you're almost there! No fresh parsley? Use dried. Out of eggs? Leave them out. Now you've no excuse not to try this terrific fish stew.

W & R

Heat butter in a large saucepan over medium heat. Add onion; cook gently, stirring until soft but not brown. Slowly stir in flour. Remove pan from heat. Break up canned tomatoes with a fork; add to flour mixture along with salt, pepper, parsley, savory, mustard and ginger. Return to heat; cover and simmer 15 minutes. Stir occasionally.

Cut fish into 1-inch / 2.5-cm cubes. Add to the sauce. Cover and simmer 10 minutes. Beat eggs in a separate bowl. Slowly add some sauce to beaten eggs, a little bit at a time, mixing well. Stir this mixture quickly into sauce and fish over low heat. Blend in lemon juice and butter. Serve in large soup bowls with hot rolls, biscuits or crackers.

SERVES 4.

Fish Burgers

Fish burgers are a delicious and healthy alternative to regular ground meat burgers. The cheese and herb centres of this variation are a pleasant surprise. When cooking fish burgers, keep in mind that fish cooks quickly. If you cook these burgers too long, they will be dry and less flavourful. We think you'll like this alternative to meat.

W & R

½ CUP	CHEDDAR CHEESE, GRATED	125 ML
¼ CUP	FRESH PARSLEY, CHOPPED	50 ML
1 TBSP	FRESH CHIVES, CHOPPED	15 ML
1 LB	HADDOCK FILLETS	450 G
1 TBSP	GREEN ONION, CHOPPED	15 ML
¾ CUP	BREADCRUMBS	175 ML
1	EGG	1
2 TBSP	CUCUMBER RELISH OR CHOPPED PICKLE	45 ML
	FLOUR FOR DUSTING	
6	HAMBURGER BUNS	6
6	LETTUCE LEAVES	6
	ALFALFA SPROUTS, SLICED TOMATO AND HERB MAYONNAISE FOR GARNISHING	

Combine the grated cheese, parsley and chives in a small bowl and mix thoroughly. Set aside.

Chop and mix fish, breadcrumbs, green onion, egg and relish in a food processor or blender until smooth. Divide mixture into 6 portions. Using your hands and a dusting of flour, take ¼ cup / 50 ml of fish mixture and flatten. Place 1 Tbsp / 15 ml of cheese and herb filling onto centre of fish mixture. Form fish mixture around the filling and pat it into a burger shape. Cook on an oiled grill over medium-high heat about 3 or 4 minutes per side until cooked through; turn once. (Burgers can also be pan-fried or microwaved on medium-high setting for about 3 minutes each side.)

Split buns; toast cut sides on grill. Place fish burgers on buns and top with lettuce, sprouts, tomato and **Herb Mayonnaise**.

SERVES 6.

½ CUP	MAYONNAISE	125 ML
1	CLOVE GARLIC, CRUSHED	1
1 TBSP	FRESH CHIVES, CHOPPED	15 ML

Combine ingredients in small bowl, stir and set aside.

MAKES ½ CUP / 125 ML.

HERBED
MAYONNAISE

Here is a variation on traditional mayonnaise that goes great on meat or fish sandwiches and burgers. Once opened, mayonnaise should be refrigerated, so be sure to keep it out of the sun and in a cool place when barbecuing.

W & R

Trout Amandine

Fresh trout still abound in the brooks and streams of the Maritimes. However, if you don't feel like swatting mosquitoes to enjoy a trout dinner, you can buy wonderful farmed trout in most fish markets. Trout is an exquisite fish that should be simply prepared. The delicate flavour is enhanced, not masked, with an amandine sauce.

W&R

4	TROUT, CLEANED	4
¼ CUP	FLOUR, SEASONED WITH SALT, PEPPER AND PAPRIKA	50 ML
1 TBSP	BUTTER	15 ML
1 TBSP	VEGETABLE OIL	15 ML

SAUCE

2 TBSP	BUTTER	30 ML
¼ CUP	SLIVERED ALMONDS	50 ML
1 TBSP	FRESH THYME, CHOPPED	15 ML
¼ CUP	FRESH PARSLEY, CHOPPED	50 ML
	JUICE OF 1 LEMON	
	LEMON WEDGES AND FRESH DILL FOR GARNISHING	

Wash trout and pat dry. Dredge fish in seasoned flour. Over medium heat, melt butter and oil in a large heavy frying pan that will accommodate 4 fish, or use 2 separate pans. When hot, lay trout in pan. Cook 4 or 5 minutes per side, turning once. The fish is done when it flakes at the touch of a fork at the thickest portion near the backbone. Place cooked trout on hot platter.

Add butter to the same frying pan and scrape brown bits from sides and base of pan as butter melts. Slowly brown butter, adding almonds and herbs. Stir well. When hot and bubbling, add lemon juice. Quickly pour sauce over trout and serve, garnished with lemon wedges and a sprig of fresh dill.

SERVES 4.

POACHED ATLANTIC SALMON

1 CUP	WHITE WINE	250 ML
1	STALK CELERY, COARSELY CHOPPED	1
2	GREEN ONIONS	2
1	BAY LEAF	1
2 TSP	PEPPERCORNS	10 ML
1 TSP	ALLSPICE	5 ML
4	SALMON STEAKS OR FILLETS, WITH OR WITHOUT SKIN	4
	RED LUMPFISH CAVIAR, LEMON WEDGES, FRESH DILL OR PARSLEY FOR GARNISHING	

Fill a shallow poaching pan with a heavy base with enough water to cover salmon. Add wine, vegetables and spices, and bring to a boil over medium heat. Reduce heat to simmer; add salmon, making sure liquid covers fish. Partially cover with lid. Simmer for approximately 8 minutes per inch / 2.5 cm thickness of fish, ensuring that the water doesn't boil. Lift fish carefully out of poaching liquid and place on warm platter or serving plates. Drizzle with **Thick and Easy Hollandaise Sauce** and dot with red lumpfish caviar for accent, if desired. Garnish with lemon wedges and sprigs of fresh dill or parsley.

SERVES 4.

Due to over-fishing and the pollution of the North American and European waterways in which wild stocks live, most of the Atlantic salmon in our fish markets is farmed, rather than wild. However, our farmed salmon is a delicious and nutritious food, highly sought throughout the world. Salmon is high in protein, and is a rich source of vitamins A and B and omega-3 oils. Poaching provides the opportunity to serve salmon hot or cold.

W&R

165
MAIN DISHES
LAND & SEA

TIP: *To determine how much water to use when poaching salmon, place uncooked salmon in poacher or pan and cover with water until desired level is reached (fish should be completely covered).*

HIGHLAND SALMON

This marinade enhances the wonderful flavour of Atlantic salmon. It will delight your dining guests, even those who avoid alcoholic beverages or don't care for the taste of Scotch whisky.

W&R

½ CUP	ORANGE JUICE	125 ML
⅓ CUP	SCOTCH WHISKY	75 ML
¼ CUP	GREEN ONIONS, CHOPPED	50 ML
⅛ CUP	MAPLE SYRUP	25 ML
1	ORANGE RIND (ZEST), GRATED	1
1 TBSP	GRAINY DIJON MUSTARD	15 ML
2 TSP	WORCESTERSHIRE SAUCE	10 ML
½ TBSP	FRESHLY GROUND BLACK PEPPER	7 ML
1 TSP	SALT	5 ML
4	FRESH, BONELESS ATLANTIC SALMON FILLETS	4
	FRESH PARSLEY SPRIGS FOR GARNISHING	

Combine orange juice, whisky, green onions, maple syrup, orange zest, mustard, Worcestershire sauce, pepper and salt in a glass mixing bowl. Place salmon fillets in a shallow glass baking dish and cover with marinade. Refrigerate 2 to 4 hours, turning fish at least once.

PREHEAT BROILER.

Remove salmon from marinade, reserving marinade. Broil salmon 4 to 5 inches / 10 to 13 cm under broiler for about 4 minutes on each side. Baste with marinade during last minute of cooking. Watch fish carefully to avoid burning, although salmon should be dark on edges. Garnish with parsley to serve.

SERVES 4.

Fresh Basil Sauce

½ CUP	WATER	125 ML
2 TSP	DIJON MUSTARD	10 ML
2 TBSP	DRY WHITE WINE	30 ML
1 TBSP	LEMON JUICE	15 ML
2½ TSP	CORNSTARCH	12 ML
1 TBSP	WATER	15 ML
½ CUP	SOUR CREAM	125 ML
2 TBSP	FRESH BASIL, CHOPPED	30 ML

Salmon and Asparagus

16	ASPARAGUS SPEARS	16
¾ LB	FRESH ATLANTIC SALMON, FILLET OR PIECES	350 G
2 TBSP	BUTTER OR MARGARINE	30 ML
1	CLOVE GARLIC, CHOPPED	1
½ LB	FRESH FETTUCINE	225 G
1 TBSP	BUTTER OR MARGARINE	15 ML
2 TBSP	FRESH OREGANO, CHOPPED	30 ML
1	FRESH LEMON, CUT IN WEDGES	1

Salmon & Asparagus Fettucine

Fresh Atlantic salmon is available across the country, and fresh asparagus can be found in supermarkets during most of the year. Combine the two with fresh herbs, toss with your favourite pasta, and you'll have dinner in thirty minutes.

W&R

Combine water, mustard, wine and lemon juice in a small saucepan and bring to a boil. Blend cornstarch and water in a small dish; stir into sauce until it boils and thickens slightly. Remove from heat. Add sour cream and basil. Mix well and set aside.

Clean asparagus; remove and discard the tough ends. Boil, steam or microwave asparagus just until tender; drain and set aside 4 whole spears, cutting the rest into 2-inch / 5-cm pieces. Keep warm.

Slice salmon fillet into thin slices, or cut pieces in half.

Heat butter in a frying pan and sauté garlic for 1 minute. Add salmon and cook, stirring gently, for about 2 minutes or until cooked through (pieces should flake easily); stir in asparagus.

Cook pasta according to directions on the package; drain and toss with butter and oregano. Place in a large bowl or in individual bowls and top with salmon and sauce. Garnish with whole asparagus spears and lemon wedges.

SERVES 4.

2 CUPS	CANNED SALMON, DRAINED AND FLAKED	500 ML
1	SMALL ONION, FINELY CHOPPED	1
½ CUP	10% CREAM OR CANNED MILK	125 ML
½ TSP	SALT	2 ML
⅛ TSP	PEPPER	.5 ML
½ TSP	SAVORY OR POULTRY SEASONING	2 ML
3	EGGS, SEPARATED	3
1 TBSP	VEGETABLE OIL	15 ML
	LEMON WEDGES FOR GARNISHING	

*M*ix salmon with onion in a medium bowl; moisten with cream. Add seasonings. Stir in egg yolks. Beat egg whites until stiff in a separate bowl then gently fold into salmon mixture.

Heat oil in a griddle or non-stick frying pan over medium heat. Drop the salmon mixture by the tablespoon onto hot surface. Cook until brown on one side, about 5 minutes; turn and cook other side about 3 minutes or until cake is cooked through.

Garnish with lemon wedges.

SERVES 4.

*S*AVOURY *S*ALMON *C*AKES

We always have several cans of salmon in our cupboard. On our honeymoon we fished salmon in Port Hardy, BC, Ross's old home town. He knew all the best fishing spots, and by early morning we were back to his mother's house with our limit. We cleaned and cooked some of the fish, but canned the rest and brought it back to the Maritimes. We use canned salmon in sandwiches, and as a salad on lettuce leaves. We especially like it in this simple recipe. *W*

Coulibiac

Coulibiac is to salmon what beef Wellington is to beef: a superb dish, well worth the extra bit of work. We've served it to raves from our guests at the Inn. Don't have the lights too dim when you present it, because half the enjoyment is in admiring the salmon surrounded by the rice, egg and mushrooms.

W&R

1½ LBS	SALMON FILLETS, SKINNED AND BONED	675 G
¼ CUP	VEGETABLE OIL	50 ML
1	BAY LEAF	1
1 TSP	THYME	5 ML
¼ CUP	FRESH PARSLEY, CHOPPED	50 ML
1 TSP	SALT	5 ML
1 TSP	FRESHLY GROUND BLACK PEPPER	5 ML
1	SMALL ONION, CHOPPED	1

Filling

3	EGGS, HARD BOILED AND SHELLED	3
1½ CUPS	WATER, BOILING	375 ML
¾ CUP	LONG-GRAIN RICE	175 ML
1 TSP	DILL	5 ML
1 TBSP	CHICKEN BOUILLON CONCENTRATE	15 ML
2 TBSP	BUTTER	30 ML
2 CUPS	MUSHROOMS, FINELY CHOPPED	470 ML
1	ONION, CHOPPED	1
¼ CUP	FRESH PARSLEY, CHOPPED	50 ML
1	PACKAGE PUFF PASTRY	1
1	EGG, BEATEN WITH A PINCH OF SALT	1

Place salmon fillets, oil, bay leaf, thyme, parsley, salt, pepper and chopped onion in a heavy-weight plastic bag. Secure bag and place in a pan to avoid dripping. Refrigerate and marinate overnight. Pour the boiling water into a saucepan. Add rice, dill and bouillon. Bring to a boil; cover and simmer on low heat 20 minutes. Cool. Place eggs and rice in refrigerator overnight.

PREHEAT OVEN TO 400° F / 200° C.

The next day, melt butter in a small frying pan over medium-high heat; sauté chopped mushrooms, onion and parsley until most of the moisture has evaporated. Let mixture cool slightly. Chop hard-boiled eggs. Roll out puff pastry into a 10 x 14-inch / 25 x 36-cm sheet on top of a slightly larger sheet of aluminum foil. Spread mushroom and onion mixture on the centre of pastry, covering an area about the size of the salmon fillets. Spread the chopped egg on top of the mixture. Spread half the rice on top of the egg. Lay the salmon fillets, head to tail, on top of the rice. Spread and mould remaining rice on top of salmon. Carefully fold pastry ends and sides up and over the salmon, using aluminum foil to assist. Seal pastry edges by brushing with beaten egg. Carefully turn pastry packet over onto a baking sheet. Remove aluminum foil. Decorate top of pastry with small pastry cutouts if you wish. Brush with beaten egg. Refrigerate for 1 or 2 hours before baking, if desired. Place in preheated oven and reduce heat to 375° F / 190° C. Bake for 25 or 30 minutes until pastry is nicely browned and you can hear contents sizzling.

SERVES 4 TO 6.

Savoury Fundy Salmon Loaf

When my grandfather bought land on the St. John River in 1905, he received the fishing rights for the portion of river in front of his land. As a child, I often helped and watched my dad haul a fresh Atlantic salmon into the boat. Back on the beach, Dad would clean and scale the fish, then we would proudly take it to Mum. She would poach or bake it. A few days later, the last bit would end up in a loaf.

W

½ CUP	BREADCRUMBS OR CRACKER CRUMBS	125 ML
2	EGGS, SLIGHTLY BEATEN	2
½ CUP	MILK	125 ML
1 LB	FRESH OR CANNED SALMON, COOKED AND FLAKED	450 G
1 TSP	LEMON JUICE	5 ML
½ TSP	SALT	2 ML
½ TSP	WORCESTERSHIRE SAUCE	2 ML
	FRESHLY GROUND BLACK PEPPER	
½ TSP	SAVORY	2 ML
2 TBSP	ONION, FINELY CHOPPED	30 ML
1 TBSP	FRESH PARSLEY, CHOPPED	15 ML
	FRESH PARSLEY AND LEMON WEDGES FOR GARNISHING	

PREHEAT OVEN 350° F / 180° C.

Combine ingredients in a large bowl in the order given. Pack firmly into a greased loaf pan and bake for 30 to 40 minutes. Let cool at least 10 minutes before serving. Slice and serve directly from the pan, or turn out onto a platter and garnish with fresh parsley and lemon wedges. Serve cold the next day with coleslaw or potato salad, or use on sandwiches with fresh lettuce or alfalfa sprouts.

SERVES 6.

Thyme & Mushroom Cream Pasta

2 Tbsp	BUTTER	30 ML
1	ONION, FINELY CHOPPED	1
1 LB	MUSHROOMS, SLICED	450 ML
1 CUP	LIGHT SOUR CREAM	250 ML
1 TSP	CHICKEN BOUILLON CONCENTRATE	5 ML
1 TSP	DIJON MUSTARD WITH SEEDS	5 ML
1 Tbsp	FRESH THYME SPRIGS	15 ML
1 LB	FRESH TOMATO PASTA	450 G

Melt butter in a frying pan and sauté onion over medium heat until soft. Add mushrooms and gently cook over medium heat until tender; avoid stirring too much as this makes mushrooms watery. Stir in sour cream, chicken bouillon and mustard; bring to a boil. Reduce heat and simmer uncovered, for 5 minutes; stir in thyme just before serving.

Cook pasta according to directions on package; drain. Spoon sauce over pasta. Sprinkle with extra thyme and pass around Parmesan cheese and the peppermill.

SERVES 4.

Fresh pasta is best, but it is often made with egg and oil, so be sure to check the list of ingredients if you're on a cholesterol-reduced diet. Dried pasta is often healthier as it contains only flour and water. This is such a flavourful, creamy sauce, it doesn't really matter which kind of pasta you use. It's also good to serve to your vegetarian friends.

W&R

Versatile Spaghetti Sauce

For families with vegetarian and non-vegetarian members, this recipe is a happy compromise. Cook the sauce first, and add the meat or seafood later.

W & R

1 Tbsp	VEGETABLE OIL	15 ML
1 CUP	ONION, CHOPPED	250 ML
½ CUP	CELERY, CHOPPED	125 ML
½ CUP	MUSHROOMS, CHOPPED	125 ML
1	CLOVE GARLIC, CHOPPED	1
¼ CUP	FRESH PARSLEY, CHOPPED	50 ML
28-OZ CAN	TOMATOES	796-ML CAN
5.5-OZ CAN	TOMATO PASTE	156-ML CAN
½ TSP	OREGANO	2 ML
½ TSP	BASIL	2 ML
½ TSP	THYME	2 ML
1 Tbsp	PAPRIKA	15 ML
1	BAY LEAF	1
2 TSP	SUGAR	10 ML
1 TSP	SALT	5 ML
½ TSP	FRESHLY GROUND BLACK PEPPER	2 ML
1 Tbsp	WORCESTERSHIRE SAUCE	15 ML
¼ CUP	SHERRY OR RED WINE	50 ML

Heat oil in a large heavy saucepan over medium heat. Add onion, celery, mushrooms, garlic and parsley; sauté, stirring occasionally, until onions are soft, about 5 minutes. Mix in canned tomatoes, breaking up any large chunks with a spoon; add remaining ingredients and cook over medium heat until mixture starts to thicken, stirring occasionally. Simmer at least 20 minutes to ensure flavours are blended. Check for seasoning; remove bay leaf.

Wonderful over any pasta with just a sprinkle of Parmesan cheese.

MAKES ABOUT 6 CUPS.

*A*fter sautéing the onions and mushrooms, push to one side in pan or remove to separate bowl and brown beef or sausage meat. Add the rest of the ingredients and cook as usual.

1 LB	MEDIUM GROUND BEEF AND/OR	450 G
½ LB	SAUSAGE MEAT OR	225 G
1 LB	SCALLOPS OR SHRIMPS, SAUTÉED AND SEASONED	450 G

Saturday Night Baked Beans

With a family of ten, Mum and Dad found beans were an economical meal. Even so, like most Maritimers, we ate them because we loved them. Saturday night just wasn't complete without Mum's baked beans and Johnnycake. On Monday we anxiously awaited noon hour and the cold bean sandwiches we knew would be in our lunch cans. Heaven.

W

TIP: *Beans, of course, can also be baked in a 350° F / 180° C oven. Generally allow 6 to 8 hours. We once baked beans on the top of our wood-burning stove. When the stove is burning all day, it's a good opportunity to make double use of the heat.*

1 CUP	DRIED SOLDIER, NAVY OR PEA BEANS	250 ML
¼ TSP	SODA	1 ML
¼ LB	SALT PORK, CUT IN SMALL CHUNKS	115 G
1	ONION, CHOPPED	1
⅛ TSP	FRESHLY GROUND BLACK PEPPER	.5 ML
1 TSP	DRY MUSTARD	5 ML
3 TBSP	BROWN SUGAR	45 ML
	OR	
¼ CUP	MAPLE SYRUP	50 ML
½ CUP	KETCHUP OR TOMATO SAUCE	125 ML
1 TBSP	BUTTER	15 ML
¼ CUP	MOLASSES	50 ML
¼ TSP	SALT	1 ML

Pick over beans to remove any pebbles or bit of dirt. Rinse well. Place beans in a large bowl, cover with about 3 inches / 8 cm water, add soda and let stand for 6 to 8 hours or overnight. To speed up the soaking stage, microwave on High until water comes to a boil, or cook in pan on top of stove until boiling and let stand 1 hour.

Fry salt pork in a lightly oiled, open pressure cooker or frying pan until nicely browned, and pour off fat. Add onion; stir while browning. Add beans, pepper, dry mustard, brown sugar or maple syrup, ketchup, butter and molasses. Pour in enough water to completely cover bean mixture. Clamp on lid of pressure cooker and bring to a boil. (Never load pressure cooker more than two-thirds full.) When pressure regulator starts to rock, reduce heat to medium-low. Cook 45 to 60 minutes. Cool cooker under cold water tap. When pressure is released, open and taste beans. Adjust seasoning and serve. Should beans require more cooking, place lid back on cooker and reheat with regulator rocking for 10 minutes. Cool and test. Beans can be served immediately. However, home-baked beans – like stews, soups and chowders – are better the second day.

SERVES 4 TO 6.

The Great Outdoors

Recipes for the
Barbecue

2 CUPS	KETCHUP	500 ML
1 CUP	WATER	250 ML
½ CUP	CIDER VINEGAR	125 ML
¾ CUP	SUGAR	175 ML
½ CUP	ONION, CHOPPED	125 ML
½ CUP	GREEN PEPPER, CHOPPED	125 ML
½ CUP	CELERY, CHOPPED	125 ML
¼ CUP	FRESH PARSLEY, CHOPPED	50 ML
2	CLOVES GARLIC, MINCED	2
3 TSP	LEMON JUICE	15 ML
⅛ TSP	TABASCO SAUCE	.5 ML
1 ½ TBSP	WORCESTERSHIRE SAUCE	25 ML
1 TSP	SALT	5 ML
½ TSP	BASIL	2 ML
½ TSP	OREGANO	2 ML
2 TBSP	BUTTER	30 ML

Herbed Barbecue Sauce

This barbecue sauce is great to have on hand when barbecuing seafood, poultry or pork. Make it ahead of time and keep it refrigerated in a closed container for up to two weeks.

W&R

Combine ketchup, water, vinegar, sugar, onion, green pepper, celery, parsley and garlic in a saucepan. Add lemon juice, Tabasco sauce, Worcestershire sauce, salt, basil, oregano and butter.

Cook over medium heat, stirring frequently for about 35 minutes until the sauce is reduced to about 4 cups.

When using this sauce with shrimp, pork or fish, wait until the last 5 minutes of cooking to apply sauce. Watch carefully to avoid burning.

MAKES ABOUT 4 CUPS.

Barbecued Beef or Pork Ribs

This rib recipe is worth putting up with several months of winter, just so you can anticipate these sizzling, succulent spareribs. Winters are long in the Maritimes, so when summer arrives, we barbecue with a vengeance.

W & R

3 TO 4 LBS	BEEF OR PORK RIBS	1.5 TO 2 KG
1	BOTTLE BEER	1
2	BAY LEAVES	2
2	LARGE ONIONS, CHOPPED	2
2	CLOVES GARLIC, CHOPPED	2
2 TBSP	VEGETABLE OIL	30 ML
½ CUP	TOMATO KETCHUP OR TOMATO SAUCE	125 ML
¼ CUP	CIDER VINEGAR	50 ML
1 TSP	PAPRIKA	5 ML
½ TSP	DRY MUSTARD	2 ML
2 TBSP	WORCESTERSHIRE SAUCE	30 ML
1 TSP	CHILI POWDER	5 ML
½ CUP	MAPLE SYRUP	125 ML
½ TSP	SALT	2 ML
	FRESHLY GROUND BLACK PEPPER	
1 TSP	THYME	5 ML

PREHEAT OVEN TO 275° F / 135° C.

Place ribs (we prefer the beef) in a large roaster with a tight-fitting lid and pour one bottle of beer over them. Add bay leaves, onions and garlic. Cover roaster with lid or use aluminum foil if lid isn't available. Place in oven for about 3 hours. This slow cooking partially cooks the ribs and keeps them moist. Remove ribs from roaster. Place them in a bowl and cover with plastic wrap to retain moisture. Skim off fat from roasting juices. Discard bay leaves; put remaining liquid into a small saucepan and add all other ingredients. Stir well over medium heat until sauce just starts to boil. Remove from stove.

Heat barbecue. When hot, place ribs on the grill and cover barbecue. Cook for 2 or 3 minutes, watching for flare-ups. Open barbecue, baste ribs with sauce and turn to grill other side. Baste again and cook for another few minutes. Turn ribs as required, so sauce does not burn. Meat should easily fall from the bones when ready to serve. Serve hot.

SERVES 4 TO 6.

4 LBS	BEEF SHORT RIBS	2 KG
½ TSP	SALT	2 ML
½ TSP	PEPPER	2 ML
1 TSP	PAPRIKA	5 ML
½ TSP	MARJORAM	2 ML
1	BAY LEAF	1
2	CLOVES GARLIC, CHOPPED	2
¼ CUP	WATER OR WINE	50 ML

Barbecued Short Ribs

Beef short ribs are a prime example of how fat provides flavour to a cut of meat. These meaty, fat-streaked ribs require longer cooking for tenderness and are often braised. This recipe combines a smoky barbecue flavour with the tenderness of braising. The ribs are barbecued first and then finished by braising in foil on top of the grill. As an added bonus, much of the fat from the ribs is lost during the initial barbecuing, but the flavour remains.

Heat barbecue to medium and oil grill. Sprinkle ribs with salt, pepper, paprika and marjoram. Place ribs bone side down on grill. Close lid and cook for 5 minutes. Watch for flare-ups. Turn ribs and continue cooking for 4 to 5 minutes per side. After about 15 to 20 minutes, when ribs are nicely browned and sizzling, remove from grill. Place ribs on double layer of heavy aluminum foil. Add red wine or water, bay leaf and garlic. Fold foil into a tightly sealed packet. Simmer gently over medium-low heat in barbecue for 1 ½ hours until meat is very tender. Open foil packet with caution.

SERVES 6.

W & R

Minted Lamb Chops

Lamb is one of our favourite meats, but we have friends who hadn't acquired a taste for it. We barbecued lamb for them and they bravely tasted these chops. It's now one of their favourite barbecue recipes.

W & R

½ CUP	CHOPPED PINE NUTS	125 ML
½ CUP	MINT LEAVES, FRESHLY CHOPPED	125 ML
⅓ CUP	VEGETABLE OIL	75 ML
2 TBSP	PARMESAN CHEESE	30 ML
¼ TSP	PEPPER, COARSELY GROUND	1 ML
1 TSP	GARLIC, FINELY CHOPPED	5 ML
6	LAMB CHOPS, 1 INCH/ 2.5 CM THICK	6
2 TBSP	VEGETABLE OIL	30 ML
	SALT AND PEPPER TO TASTE	

Clean and oil grill. If using coals, heat until they are ash white. Heat a gas barbecue to medium-high.

Stir together the pine nuts, mint, oil Parmesan cheese, pepper and garlic; set aside. Brush lamb chops with vegetable oil and sprinkle lightly with salt and pepper. Place on barbecue. Grill, basting with oil and turning occasionally for 10 to 15 minutes. Spoon 1 Tbsp / 15 ml mint sauce on each lamb chop. Serve with **Grilled Tomatoes and Eggplant**, **Barbecued Potatoes** and **Barbecue Bread**.

SERVES 6.

3 LB	CHICKEN PIECES	1.5 KG
	SALT AND PEPPER	
¼ CUP	VEGETABLE OIL	50 ML
2	CLOVES FRESH GARLIC, CHOPPED	2
1 TSP	OREGANO	5 ML
1 TSP	THYME	5 ML
1 TSP	PAPRIKA	5 ML

GRILLED CHICKEN

Place chicken pieces in a round, microwave-safe glass dish or pie plate and season with salt and pepper. Pierce chicken several times with a fork or knife.

Mix oil, garlic and herbs in a separate bowl. Pour mixture over chicken, ensuring that all parts are well covered. Cover with clear plastic wrap; allow venting by piercing a hole in the wrap. Microwave on high for 15 minutes, turning pieces at least twice during this pre-cooking stage. Let chicken rest for 15 minutes while barbecue is heating.

Oil grill and place chicken pieces over medium-high heat. Cook with barbecue lid closed and watch for flare-ups which should be doused with a squirt from a water bottle. Turn chicken when it is nicely browned, about 3 to 5 minutes. Baste with your favourite barbecue sauce. Cook another 3 to 5 minutes, turn again, baste and cook only another minute or two before serving. Check to see if chicken is completely done by piercing it with a knife or fork; the juices should run clear. If you have a meat thermometer, the chicken should have reached an internal temperature of 185° F / 85° C.

SERVES 4.

As a novice barbecue chef in the sixties, I found chicken to be a formidable challenge to cook properly on the grill. I knew that poultry must always be thoroughly cooked. But I also learned, to my disappointment, that to cook raw chicken completely on the grill required lots of time and often resulted in meat that was dry and charred. Imagine my delight when I found that pre-cooking chicken pieces in the microwave oven allowed them to be finished quickly and to a crispy, golden brown on the grill.

R

183
THE GREAT OUTDOORS

TIP: *Baste the chicken only during the last 5 minutes of cooking. This keeps sweet, fruity or tomato sauces from burning but allows their flavours to penetrate the poultry.*

Greek Chicken Grill

Ever since I spent some time in the Mediterranean while on a newspaper assignment with the United Nations Forces in Cyprus, I've had a profound respect for Middle Eastern cooking. The wonderful sunny flavours of fresh lemon, olive oil, thyme, rosemary and garlic always evoke the Mediterranean warmth. The following marinade can be used for lamb or pork as well as chicken.

R

4	BONELESS CHICKEN BREASTS	4
¼ CUP	OLIVE OIL	50 ML
2 TBSP	LEMON JUICE	30 ML
1 TBSP	LEMON PEEL (ZEST), GRATED	15 ML
1	CLOVE GARLIC, DICED	1
1 TSP	THYME	5 ML
1 TSP	ROSEMARY LEAVES, CRUSHED	5 ML

Using a sharp knife, carefully score chicken breasts diagonally on one side no deeper than half way through the thickness of the meat. Lay breasts in a shallow glass baking dish. Mix oil, lemon juice, zest, garlic and herbs in a small glass bowl. Pour mixture over chicken and rub well into the meat. Cover with plastic wrap and marinate in refrigerator for about 1 hour. Remove from refrigerator and turn breasts over, ensuring that both sides are well coated with marinade. Let stand at room temperature while barbecue is heating to medium-high. Oil grill. Place breast fillets on grill and close lid of barbecue. Cook for 12 to 15 minutes, turning once. Serve with rice.

SERVES 4.

GRILLED OYSTERS

24	OYSTERS, LIVE IN SHELLS	24
2	LEMONS, CUT INTO WEDGES	2
	FRESHLY GROUND BLACK PEPPER	
	WORCESTERSHIRE SAUCE	

Heat barbecue to medium-high. Open lid and lay oysters on the grill, shell and all. Carefully place them so the bottom shell lays flat and will hold the oyster when cooked. Close the grill lid and cook for about 6 or 7 minutes until oysters pop open. As the oysters open, carefully remove them one at a time from the grill with tongs or oven mitts. Place them on a platter and surround with lemon wedges. Have the pepper mill and Worcestershire sauce handy for those who might want it. Once the shells have cooled sufficiently to allow easy handling, squeeze on some lemon juice if you wish and suck the oysters and the heavenly nectar right from the shells.

SERVES 4 TO 6.

We've always refused to get into a debate on where the best oysters in the world are found. Whenever asked that question, the answer we find most gratifying is "The best oysters in the world are right here on our plate." Oysters are fantastic raw, just as God made them. However, for those who like their seafood cooked, here is a quick and easy way to make great barbecue appetizers prior to the big cook-out.

W&R

TIP: *Oysters in the shell should be freshly harvested and all the shells should be tightly closed. Discard any that are partially open and don't close when handled. Wash the sand or grit off the outside of the shells.*

Honey-Garlic Shrimp

The combination of garlic, honey and soy sauce makes a wonderful glaze or marinade for pork, chicken, beef and several types of fish and seafood. Here is a slight variation on the teriyaki theme that makes shrimp a giant pleaser.

W&R

2 TBSP	LIGHT SOY SAUCE	30 ML
1 TBSP	HOISIN SAUCE	15 ML
1 TBSP	BARBECUE SAUCE	15 ML
1 TSP	CHILI SAUCE	5 ML
1 TBSP	HONEY	15 ML
1 TBSP	VEGETABLE OIL	15 ML
1 TBSP	DRY SHERRY	15 ML
2	CLOVES GARLIC, CRUSHED	2
2 LBS	UNCOOKED SHRIMP, SHELLED	1 KG

Combine sauces, honey, oil, sherry and garlic in a large bowl; add shrimp and mix well. Cover and refrigerate for 2 hours. Put shrimp on skewers. Barbecue on a hot grill 1 to 2 minutes per side until tender, occasionally brushing with marinade.

SERVES 4.

TIP: *When barbecuing with wood skewers, soak them in water for about ½ hour before using.*

6 Tbsp	OLIVE OR VEGETABLE OIL, OR A MIXTURE OF BOTH OILS	90 ml
1	CLOVE GARLIC, CHOPPED	1
1 tsp	GINGER ROOT, GRATED	5 ml
1 Tbsp	FRESH PARSLEY, CHOPPED	15 ml
	SPRINKLE OF SUGAR	
	SPRINKLE OF SALT	
¾ lb	FRESH SHRIMP, SHELLED	375 g
¾ lb	SCALLOPS	375 g
	BREADCRUMBS	

SKEWERED SHRIMP & SCALLOPS

Shrimp and scallops are great barbecued because they take so little time to cook. The shrimp should turn pink and the scallops an opaque white when cooked. Oil your barbecue grill well before placing the seafood skewers on it.

W&R

PREHEAT BROILER OR GRILL.

Combine oil, garlic, ginger, parsley and seasoning in a large glass mixing bowl and mix well. Wash scallops, discarding any broken shells. Add shrimp and scallops to marinade and mix to coat.

Sprinkle with just enough breadcrumbs to lightly coat shrimp and scallops. Marinate for about 30 minutes. Thread shimp and scallops alternately on skewers, bending shrimp in a "U" shape. Place on an oiled grill over medium-high heat. Broil quickly about 2 minutes; turn and broil other side for 2 minutes. Serve hot. Delicious as an appetizer or main course with saffron rice.

SERVES 10 AS AN APPETIZER OR 4 AS A MAIN COURSE.

Spicy Honey-Glazed Mussels

Fresh mussels are cultivated locally throughout the Maritimes. They are available year round, and form the basis for an inexpensive and nutritious meal. Don't ignore mussels for your barbecue, especially in this delicious recipe.

W&R

2 LBS	MUSSELS	1 KG
½ LB	BACON	225 G
2 TBSP	HONEY	30 ML
2 TBSP	TOMATO SAUCE	30 ML
1 TSP	WORCESTERSHIRE SAUCE	5 ML
¼ TSP	TABASCO SAUCE	1 ML

Briefly steam mussels in large saucepan of salted water until shells open, about 5 minutes after the water begins to boil. Remove mussels from shells, discarding any that did not open. Cut bacon into 1 x 2½-inch / 2.5 x 6-cm strips. Wrap mussels in bacon and thread onto skewers. Place skewers in a single layer in dish. Mix honey, tomato sauce, Worcestershire sauce and Tabasco sauce in a small glass bowl and brush on skewered mussels. Marinate in refrigerator for about 1 hour.

Remove skewers from dish and barbecue or grill until bacon is crisp, brushing occasionally with remaining glaze.

SERVES 4 TO 6.

TIP: *Mussels may be wrapped in bacon, threaded onto skewers and marinated overnight in refrigerator.*

Barbecued Halibut

¼ CUP	LEMON JUICE	50 ML
2 TBSP	FRESH DILL, CHOPPED	30 ML
2 TBSP	VEGETABLE OR OLIVE OIL	30 ML
2 TBSP	GRAINY DIJON MUSTARD	30 ML
	SALT AND PEPPER TO TASTE	
1 LB	FRESH HALIBUT STEAKS OR FILLETS	450 G
	LEMON WEDGES FOR GARNISHING	

Combine lemon juice, dill, oil, mustard and seasonings in a large shallow bowl. Add fish, coating well. Cover and place in refrigerator for at least 30 minutes or up to 2 hours. Baste and turn occasionally.

Remove fish from marinade; reserve sauce. Place fish on an oiled grill over medium-high heat. Cook, turning and basting with sauce for about 8 minutes per inch / 2.5 cm thickness of fish. When fish appears opaque and flakes when tested with fork, remove from grill and garnish with fresh lemon wedges.

SERVES 4.

Halibut, a member of the flatfish family, is readily available in the Maritimes. The delicate flavour of this white-fleshed fish belies its potentially massive size. Usually harvested when less than 100 lbs / 50 kg, the meat is low in fat and must be cooked quickly to avoid dryness. This lemon-mustard marinade helps the fish stay moist, but be careful not to overcook it.

W & R

Maple-Barbecued Salmon

Maple syrup and salmon are an unusual but wonderful combination, whether united on the barbecue or in the smoke house. Spicy but sweet with a slightly smoky flavour from the grill, maple-glazed salmon is reminiscent of the many salmon I've smoked over the years. This barbecue recipe provides the wonderful flavour of maple smoked salmon without the smokehouse fire.   *R*

1 CUP	MAPLE SYRUP	250 ML
1	SMALL ONION, CHOPPED	1
2 Tbsp	CIDER VINEGAR	30 ML
2 Tbsp	WORCESTERSHIRE SAUCE	30 ML
1 TO 2 TSP	HOT PEPPER SAUCE	5 TO 10 ML
1 TSP	SALT	5 ML
1 TSP	DRY MUSTARD	5 ML
4	SALMON FILLETS, BONELESS WITH SKIN ATTACHED	4

*P*repare sauce by combining maple syrup, onion, vinegar, Worcestershire sauce, pepper sauce, salt and mustard in a small saucepan over medium heat. Bring to a boil, stirring constantly. Reduce heat and simmer for 4 to 5 minutes. Remove sauce from heat and cool. Sauce may be cooled and stored in a sealed container in the refrigerator for about 10 days.

Heat the barbecue to medium-high. Place salmon fillets, skin side down, on an oiled grill. Using a pastry or barbecue brush, paint maple syrup mixture on salmon. Close the lid of the barbecue and cook for 3 to 4 minutes, keeping watch for flare-ups. Raise the lid of the barbecue and cook fillets for another 2 to 3 minutes. Carefully lift each fillet with a spatula, turn once, and grill for 1 more minute, or until the salmon flakes easily. Remove fillets from barbecue and serve on a hot platter.

SERVES 4.

TIP: *This sauce may also be used to finish barbecued pork or poultry.*

VEGETABLES

| 2 LBS | MIXED VEGETABLES (CARROTS, SMALL ONIONS, PARSNIPS, TURNIPS, POTATOES, ZUCCHINI, SWEET PEPPERS, TOMATOES, SQUASH OR EGGPLANT) | 900 G |

MARINADE

¼ CUP	VEGETABLE OR OLIVE OIL	50 ML
1 TBSP	LEMON RIND (ZEST), GRATED	15 ML
2 TBSP	FRESH CHIVES OR GREEN ONIONS, CHOPPED	30 ML
5	CLOVES GARLIC, MINCED	5
1 TSP	OREGANO OR THYME, OR BOTH	5 ML
½ TSP	SALT	2 ML
¼ TSP	PEPPER	1 ML

GRILLED VEGETABLES

This is a great way to include vegetables in your next barbecue and have them taste like they are a part of the barbecue and not an afterthought from the kitchen stove.

W&R

Wash vegetables and peel those that require peeling. Leave most small vegetables whole, and cut only larger ones into common portion sizes. Potatoes, onions, carrots and parsnips can be cut in half, while turnip, zucchini, squash and eggplant should be cut into large 1-inch / 2.5-cm slices. Partially cook potatoes, carrots, parsnips and turnips by boiling them in salted water for 5 to 8 minutes. (If you have a microwave oven, place vegetables on a microwave-safe dish, cover with plastic wrap and cook 5 to 6 minutes on high.)

Mix marinade ingredients in a large bowl. Add partially cooked vegetables and shake to coat. Reserve marinade. Thread vegetables on skewers or place directly on an oiled grill over medium-high heat; cook, turning occasionally and brushing with reserved marinade until most vegetables are crisp on the outside and heated through.

By carefully turning vegetables with a spatula, you can arrange them so the hot grill decoratively marks their surfaces.

SERVES 4.

COBBED CORN IN THE CAN

Here is a barbecue recipe that I discovered when spending a summer with friends the year of my high-school graduation. I had always enjoyed a corn boil, but had never had corn on the cob cooked on a barbecue. Even more unique was the novel way in which the ears of cooked corn were buttered. If you don't want to barbecue your corn, at least try the fancy buttering method.

R

12	EARS SWEET CORN, FRESHLY HUSKED	12
2 TSP	SALT	10 ML
1 TSP	PEPPER	5 ML
1 TSP	PAPRIKA	5 ML
3 CUPS	HOT WATER	750 ML
½ CUP	BUTTER	125 ML

Dip each husked cob of corn in fresh water; carefully lay it on a sheet of aluminum foil large enough to completely wrap the cob. Mix salt, pepper and paprika; sprinkle corn lightly with mixed spices. Wrap foil tightly round corn, twisting the ends to seal. Lay foil-wrapped cobs on a hot grill.

Place a large empty 48-oz / 1.5-litre juice can, with the top removed, on grill. Pour hot water into can and add butter. Cook corn 18 to 20 minutes, turning frequently while cooking. Carefully unwrap one cob to test for doneness. (Corn should be moist, tender and steaming hot.) Before eating corn, carefully push each ear into juice can until liquid rises almost to top of can. When the corn is removed, it will be left with a thin coating of melted butter. This is a great way to efficiently butter many cobs of corn.

SERVES 6 TO 8.

1	SMALL EGGPLANT	1	
	SALT		
3	TOMATOES, HALVED	3	
1 Tbsp	VEGETABLE OIL	15 ml	
½ tsp	OREGANO	2 ml	
	PEPPER		
2 Tbsp	PARMESAN CHEESE, FRESHLY GRATED	30 ml	

Cut eggplant into ¼-inch / 5-mm slices; place in a colander and sprinkle with salt. Let stand 30 minutes.

Rinse eggplant under cold water; pat dry. Brush with oil, sprinkle with oregano and pepper. Place on grill; cook for about 10 minutes, turning occasionally, until tender but not charred.

After eggplant has been cooking 5 minutes, place tomato halves on grill and spoon about 1 tsp / 5 ml Parmesan cheese on each half. Cook about 5 minutes (depending on size of tomato) or until heated through.

SERVES 6.

GRILLED TOMATOES & EGGPLANT

Men and women both love barbecuing, but for different reasons. For men it brings out the macho feelings of providing for the family. Then there's the primal thrill of taking raw meat outdoors and returning with it cooked to a turn, and the compliments from everyone at the dinner table. Women love it because there are no pots or pans to clean. Here's a great vegetable recipe to try the next time the barbecue is hot.

W & R

Barbecued Potatoes

Everyone loves potatoes. Ross's mother doesn't feel she's had dinner if there are no potatoes. And when Ross makes this recipe, he always has to double it because everyone comes back for seconds. If your family is tired of the same old mashed or boiled potatoes, take an extra few minutes and try this recipe. In the winter, use the oven.

W

6 OR 8	LARGE NEW POTATOES	6 OR 8
3 TBSP	VEGETABLE OR OLIVE OIL	45 ML
	GENEROUS SHAKES OF: PAPRIKA, THYME AND ROSEMARY	
	SALT AND PEPPER TO TASTE	
	GARLIC POWDER TO TASTE	

While barbecue is heating, scrub potatoes, leaving on skins. Cut spuds in half lengthwise and toss them in oil. Shake dried spices and herbs on oiled potatoes and toss once again. Place in a baking dish and microwave on high for about 10 or 12 minutes until potatoes are just starting to get fork tender. Remove from microwave and place on hot grill in barbecue. Cover and bake for a few minutes. Turn, being careful not to burn them. Continue roasting until golden brown and soft to the fork.

SERVES 6 TO 8.

BARBECUED BREAD

1	LOAF FRENCH OR ITALIAN BREAD	1
½ CUP	BUTTER OR MARGARINE	125 ML
½ CUP	CHEDDAR CHEESE, GRATED	125 ML
¼ CUP	MOZZARELLA CHEESE, GRATED	50 ML
2 TSP	PAPRIKA	10 ML
1 TBSP	MARJORAM	15 ML
1	CLOVE GARLIC, FINELY CHOPPED	1
1 TSP	FRESHLY GROUND BLACK PEPPER	5 ML

If bread is not sliced, slice it in ¾-inch / 2-cm slices. In a small bowl, mix butter, cheese and spices. Spread bread slices with mixture and restore to loaf shape, wrapping loaf with aluminum foil. Seal top seam and end of foil packet to retain moisture as butter melts. Lay bread on hot grill, turning frequently for 15 minutes. Remove foil carefully from steaming bread and serve.

SERVES 12.

I was a barbecue purist at one time, believing that food should not be wrapped in foil if it was to be cooked on the grill. And although now I recognize that some food can be cooked on the grill in foil for convenience sake, I try to avoid doing so. One of the main benefits of barbecue cooking is the smoky flavour and taste imparted by the open flame. Most foil-wrapped foods don't gain this. That being said, the two exceptions I make are corn on the cob and barbecued bread.

R

Celebrating the Harvest

Vegetable Side Dishes

ASPARAGUS WITH MUSTARD & LEMON SAUCE

12 TO 16	ASPARAGUS SPEARS	12 TO 16
2 TBSP	BUTTER	30 ML
1 TBSP	GRAINY DIJON MUSTARD	15 ML
¼ CUP	18% CREAM	50 ML
2 TSP	LEMON RIND (ZEST), GRATED	10 ML
	SALT TO TASTE	
	PINCH OF CAYENNE	

Steam or boil asparagus until tender, about 5 minutes. Drain and set aside.

Melt butter in a small saucepan and stir in mustard and cream, mixing well until hot. Add half of the lemon zest and salt to taste. Pour over asparagus. Garnish with remaining lemon zest and a pinch of cayenne. Serve hot.

SERVES 4.

If you have even the smallest plot of land, grow asparagus. Plant them once, and every spring when you're picking daffodils and tulips for your table, you can be harvesting a feast of fresh asparagus. Is anything as satisfying as veggies fresh from the garden?

W & R

199
CELEBRATING THE HARVEST

TIP: *Cooking asparagus in tall pots to accommodate the height of the vegetable was trendy a few years ago, but we now find that placing the stalks in a frying pan with about ½ inch/1 cm of lightly salted water works just fine. Watch the pan carefully: it doesn't take long to boil dry.*

Orange-Glazed Beets

We really like beets, buttered, pickled or Harvard, but this is a special dining experience.

W & R

2 CUPS	FRESHLY COOKED OR CANNED BEETS	500 ML
2 TBSP	BUTTER	30 ML
¼ CUP	ORANGE JUICE	50 ML
1 TBSP	ORANGE MARMALADE	15 ML
1 TSP	THYME	5 ML
	FRESHLY GRATED BLACK PEPPER TO TASTE	
	ORANGE RIND (ZEST), GRATED, FOR GARNISHING	

Melt butter in a small saucepan. Add beets and gently heat through. Mix orange juice, marmalade and thyme in a small bowl. Pour over beets and boil gently, uncovered, until mixture thickens, stirring to prevent sticking. Add pepper to taste and serve hot with orange zest as garnish.

SERVES 4.

½ LB	BRUSSELS SPROUTS	225 G
1 TBSP	BUTTER	15 ML
1	CLOVE GARLIC, CHOPPED	1
¼ CUP	CHOPPED PECANS	50 ML

BRUSSELS SPROUTS WITH GARLIC PECANS

Wash sprouts and remove damaged outer leaves. Trim ends and score bottoms with an X to assure even cooking. Cook sprouts in a saucepan of lightly salted water over medium heat for 15 minutes or until tender. Drain, add butter and chopped garlic, and sauté briefly to blend flavours. Sprinkle with chopped pecans and serve.

SERVES 4.

Brussels sprouts are a member of the cabbage family and one of our favourite vegetables. They are best when freshly harvested in the fall, but we enjoy them all year round. Great with just a squeeze of fresh lemon, they become very special when prepared with garlic and pecans.

W & R

Red Cabbage with Apples

We've had guests who had never eaten cooked cabbage enjoy this recipe so much, they've asked for seconds. A real winner.

W & R

2 Tbsp	VEGETABLE OIL	30 ML
1	ONION, COARSELY CHOPPED	1
¼ CUP	CIDER VINEGAR	50 ML
2 Tbsp	BROWN SUGAR OR HONEY	30 ML
	SALT AND PEPPER TO TASTE	
1	GREEN APPLE, CORED AND THINLY SLICED	1
1	SMALL RED CABBAGE, COARSELY SHREDDED	1

Heat oil in a large frying pan. Add onion and sauté until softened, about 5 minutes. Stir in vinegar, sugar, salt and pepper to taste.

Add apple and cabbage. Bring liquid to a boil; reduce heat to medium, cover and cook until cabbage wilts, about 10 minutes. Stir occasionally to coat cabbage with vinegar-sugar mixture.

Serve as an accompaniment to pan-fried bratwurst or baked spareribs and oven-roasted potatoes.

SERVES 6.

2	EGGPLANTS	2	
¼ CUP	VEGETABLE OIL	50	ML
½ CUP	ONION, CHOPPED	125	ML
¼ CUP	GREEN PEPPER, CHOPPED	50	ML
1	CLOVE GARLIC, MINCED	1	
2	TOMATOES, QUARTERED	2	
1 CUP	MUSHROOMS, SLICED	250	ML
2 TSP	FRESH OREGANO, CHOPPED	10	ML
2 TSP	FRESH BASIL, CHOPPED	10	ML
½ TSP	SALT	2	ML
	PEPPER TO TASTE		
¼ CUP	FRESH PARSLEY, CHOPPED	50	ML

STUFFED BAKED EGGPLANT

We're all familiar with the large, purple eggplant known as Western eggplant. However, there are now about ten varieties of eggplant available in specialty stores. They range in colour from pink and purple to ivory and black. Some are as small as cherries; others are as big as melons. All varieties have a somewhat bland taste and require the use of garlic, peppers and herbs to spice up their flavour. This recipe calls for the common Western eggplant.

W & R

203
CELEBRATING
THE HARVEST

HEAT OVEN TO 350° F / 180° C.

Cut eggplant in half lengthwise; remove and dice pulp, leaving ¼-inch / 5-mm shell. Place eggplant halves in a 13 x 9-inch / 3.5-litre baking pan. Set aside.

Heat oil in frying pan and add onion, green pepper, garlic, diced eggplant, tomatoes, mushrooms, oregano, basil, salt and pepper. Cook over medium heat about 3 to 5 minutes until heated through; stir frequently. Spoon into eggplant shells; sprinkle with fresh parsley. Bake 30 to 35 minutes until eggplant is fork tender.

SERVES 4.

EGGPLANT PARMIGIANO

As a young bride, I was introduced to many exotic vegetables by my father-in-law, who loved to shop. He also loved a bargain, and used to visit the produce department of the supermarkets just before closing on Saturday night. He would talk the produce manager into selling him vegetables or fruit that wouldn't last until Monday. When he brought me my first eggplant, the only cookbook I owned that had a recipe for this unusual, pear-shaped vegetable was *The Joy of Cooking*. We've come a long way!

W

2	EGGPLANTS	2
	LIGHTLY SALTED WATER	
2	EGGS	2
1 TSP	SALT	5 ML
¼ TSP	PEPPER	1 ML
2 TBSP	VEGETABLE OIL	30 ML
1	GARLIC CLOVE, MINCED	1
1 TSP	THYME, FRESHLY CHOPPED	5 ML
2 CUPS	TOMATO SAUCE	500 ML
½ LB	MOZZARELLA CHEESE, THINLY SLICED	250 G
¼ CUP	PARMESAN CHEESE, GRATED	50 ML

PREHEAT OVEN TO 350° F / 180° C.

Peel eggplants and then slice them ¼ inch / 5 mm thick. Cover with lightly salted water and soak for about half an hour. Dry with a paper towel.

Lightly beat eggs in a bowl and season with salt and pepper. Dip eggplant slices in mixture. Heat oil in a frying pan over medium heat and quickly fry both sides of eggplant until lightly browned. Drain on a paper towel.

Mix garlic and thyme with tomato sauce. In a 13 x 9-inch / 3.5-litre baking pan, arrange layers of eggplant, tomato sauce, mozzarella and Parmesan cheese. Bake, uncovered, for 30 minutes or until bubbly and heated through.

SERVES 4 TO 6.

1	BUTTERCUP SQUASH, PEELED AND CUBED	1
¼ TSP	ORANGE PEEL (ZEST), GRATED	1 ML
2 TBSP	ORANGE JUICE	30 ML
¼ CUP	BUTTER OR MARGARINE	50 ML
2 TBSP	BROWN SUGAR	30 ML
½ TSP	SALT	2 ML
	DASH OF NUTMEG	

Steam or boil squash until tender. Remove from heat and mash. Add two cups of squash to a large pan along with remaining ingredients. Mix well and cook over low heat for 5 minutes, stirring occasionally.

SERVES 4.

WINTER SQUASH WITH ORANGE

Winter squash becomes starchy and dry as it waits in a cool, dry place to be retrieved, cooked and eaten. We have a closet at the Inn that is perfect for storing squash. Fortunately, we also have understanding guests who don't mind sharing this space. We buy at least a bushel of squash every September at Horse Farming Days held at Carter's Point on the Kingston Peninsula.

W & R

205
CELEBRATING
THE HARVEST

TIP: *To make preparing squash easier, pierce the skin with a fork and microwave for 5 minutes or until the skin becomes soft. It will then peel easily. Squash microwaves well either whole or in wedges. Allow 4 to 5 minutes for each potato-sized wedge.*

Mashed Turnips with Carrots & Orange in Mushroom Caps

Adding mashed carrots to turnips mellows the turnip and adds flavour to the carrots. And serving them in mushroom caps adds pizzazz to any plate.

W & R

1	SMALL YELLOW TURNIP	1
4	CARROTS	4
1 Tbsp	BUTTER	15 ML
2 Tbsp	BROWN SUGAR	30 ML
2 Tbsp	ORANGE JUICE CONCENTRATE	30 ML
	PINCH OF NUTMEG (OPTIONAL)	
	SALT AND FRESHLY GROUND PEPPER TO TASTE	
1 Tbsp	VEGETABLE OIL	15 ML
16	LARGE WHITE MUSHROOMS	16
2 Tbsp	FRESH PARSLEY, CHOPPED	30 ML

Peel turnip and carrots. Cut into small chunks and cook in lightly salted water until tender; drain and mash with butter. Stir in sugar, orange juice concentrate, nutmeg and salt and pepper to taste.

While vegetables are cooking, clean mushrooms with a damp cloth and remove stems. Heat oil in a frying pan over medium heat and sauté caps until golden brown. Set aside, keeping warm.

Fill each mushroom cap with vegetable mixture and sprinkle with chopped parsley. Serve immediately or keep warm in a low oven. Place 2 caps on each plate.

SERVES 8.

1½ CUPS	FLOUR	375 ML
1 TBSP	SUGAR	15 ML
1 TBSP	BAKING POWDER	15 ML
½ TSP	SALT	2 ML
1	EGG, BEATEN	1
1 TBSP	MOLASSES	15 ML
1¾ CUPS	MILK OR BUTTERMILK	425 ML
2 TBSP	VEGETABLE OIL	30 ML
1 CUP	WHOLE KERNEL CORN OR CREAMED CORN	250 ML

CORN FRITTERS

Sift or blend together dry ingredients in a large bowl. Beat the egg, molasses, milk and oil in a separate bowl; add to dry ingredients, mixing only until combined. Fold in the drained whole kernel corn or creamed corn (or a combination of the two).

Heat a heavy griddle or frying pan until drops of water dance across it. Lightly oil. Pour ¼ cup / 50 ml of batter onto griddle for each 4-inch / 10-cm fritter. Fry until edge of fritter begins to dry and lose its gloss. Turn over and fry until golden brown.

MAKES ABOUT 18 FRITTERS. SERVES 6.

Corn fritters were a special supper dish Mum prepared for us when we were kids. She made them small and served them three at a time. The poor woman could never make enough! Mum wouldn't sit down with us; she would stand at the stove frying as fast as she could, dropping fritters onto our waiting plates. Generously spread with butter and molasses, we dug into them with more relish than if she had given us steak or lobster. I enjoy them just as much today.

W

Fiddlehead Soufflé

When I first came to the Maritimes from British Columbia, I couldn't wait to try fiddle-heads. These succulent little ostrich ferns are plucked from their moist beds barely after they've raised their heads to the spring sunshine. Once a truly unique east coast delicacy, fiddleheads have now swept the country in popularity. They're great on their own with just a little lemon juice and butter but they're even more *eggciting* in this soufflé.

R

TIP: *To make buttered breadcrumbs, melt 1 Tbsp / 15 ml butter in a small frying pan; add ½ cup / 125 ml breadcrumbs and stir over medium heat about 5 minutes until crumbs are well coated with butter and lightly browned.*

1 LB	FIDDLEHEADS	450 G
4 TBSP	BUTTER	60 ML
3 TBSP	FLOUR	45 ML
1 CUP	MILK	250 ML
4	EGGS, SEPARATED	4
1 CUP	CHEDDAR CHEESE, GRATED	250 ML
1 TSP	SALT	5 ML
¼ TSP	CREAM OF TARTAR	1 ML
1 TSP	WORCESTERSHIRE SAUCE	5 ML
2 TBSP	BREADCRUMBS, BUTTERED	30 ML

PREHEAT OVEN TO 375° F / 190° C.

Wash fiddleheads and trim off dark ends. Cook in a saucepan in lightly salted boiling water for no longer than 2 minutes. Drain and set aside.

Make a white sauce by melting butter in a heavy saucepan; mix in flour and stir over low heat for 1 or 2 minutes. Slowly stir in milk, whisking until well blended and smooth. Beat in egg yolks one at a time. Add grated cheese and ¾ tsp / 3 ml salt; cook until thickened. Remove from heat and set aside.

Beat egg whites in a separate bowl until foamy; add cream of tartar. Continue beating until stiff, but not dry. Blend in remaining salt and Worcestershire sauce. Gently fold egg whites into egg yolk mixture, add warm fiddleheads, and place mixture in a lightly greased 6-cup / 1.5-litre mould or soufflé dish. Smooth with spatula and sprinkle with buttered breadcrumbs. Bake 25 to 30 minutes or until golden brown; a knife inserted in the side of soufflé should come out clean. Be careful not to open oven door during first 20 minutes of baking.

SERVES 4 TO 6.

Maple-Glazed Fiddleheads & Cranberries

¼ CUP	BUTTER	50 ML
¼ LB	FIDDLEHEADS	115 G
¼ CUP	FRESH OR FROZEN CRANBERRIES	50 ML
2 TBSP	MAPLE SYRUP	30 ML
	SALT AND PEPPER TO TASTE	

Melt butter in a large frying pan over medium-high heat. Add cleaned fiddleheads and sauté for 3 minutes or until they begin to change colour. Stir in cranberries and maple syrup. Cover, reduce heat to medium and steam for 3 more minutes or until tender, but crisp. Season to taste.

SERVES 2.

Maple trees are tapped in late winter, while the snow is still on the ground. Fiddleheads are harvested in early spring, just as the flooded rivers begin to ebb. Cranberries are picked in the fall from flooded bogs. So, how do you coordinate the three for cooking? Simply freeze the fresh vegetable or fruit and use them, together with bottled maple syrup, whenever you like. This recipe is especially nice at Christmas.

W & R

209
CELEBRATING
THE HARVEST

Fiddlehead Salad with New Potatoes

We're fortunate to have easy access to fiddleheads and potatoes, both of which grow in abundance. We enjoy the little, new potatoes many farmers don't bother harvesting. Given the opportunity, we gladly take our baskets and pick all the small leftovers. They're perfect in this recipe.

W & R

16	SMALL NEW POTATOES (OR 8 LARGE POTATOES, CUT IN HALF)	16
½ LB	FRESH GREEN BEANS	225 G
1 LB	FIDDLEHEADS, CLEANED AND TRIMMED	450 G
⅓ CUP	VEGETABLE OIL	75 ML
¼ CUP	RED WINE VINEGAR	50 ML
½ TSP	SALT	2 ML
½ TSP	COARSELY GROUND BLACK PEPPER	2 ML
2 TBSP	DIJON MUSTARD	30 ML
1	HEAD ROMAINE, RINSED, DRIED AND TORN	1
2 TSP	SESAME SEEDS, TOASTED	10 ML

Cook potatoes in lightly salted water for 12 to 15 minutes, until fork tender. Set aside. Cook beans for 10 to 15 minutes, until crispy tender. Cook fiddleheads for 5 to 6 minutes until crispy tender. Place beans and fiddleheads in ice water to chill. Drain. Whisk together oil, vinegar, salt, pepper and mustard in a small bowl. Pour 2 Tbsp / 30 ml dressing over cooled potatoes; toss to coat. Place lettuce on a serving platter; arrange potatoes, beans and fiddleheads on leaves. Drizzle with ¼ cup / 50 ml dressing; sprinkle with toasted sesame seeds. Serve with remaining dressing on the side. For a picnic, pack dressing in a bottle and add it when you are ready to eat.

SERVES 8.

Herbed Baked Potatoes

4	POTATOES (NEW ARE BEST)	4
2 TBSP	BUTTER	30 ML
2 TBSP	VEGETABLE OIL	30 ML
1 TSP	GARLIC, CHOPPED	5 ML
1 TSP	PARSLEY, CHOPPED	5 ML
¼ TSP	OREGANO	1 ML
¼ TSP	THYME	1 ML
	PAPRIKA	
	PARMESAN CHEESE	

These baked potatoes have a rich and interesting flavour; they also look very attractive.

W & R

PREHEAT OVEN TO 400° F / 200° C.

Wash potatoes. Remove any dark spots or blemishes. Lay potato alongside wooden spoon handle. Cut ¼-inch / 5-mm slices across potato allowing spoon handle to stop knife from cutting all the way through. Melt butter in a dish and add oil. Place potatoes in a shallow baking dish and drizzle with oil and butter mixture. Sprinkle with herbs and bake 35 minutes until almost done. Sprinkle with paprika and Parmesan cheese; finish baking 10 minutes or until lightly browned and cooked through.

SERVES 4.

TIP: *If a whole potato is too much, or if your potatoes are quite large, cut the potatoes in half, lengthwise, slice them as you would a whole potato and proceed with the recipe.*

POTATOES DUCHESS

Here in the Maritimes, we eat a lot of potatoes. However, even those of us who want potatoes with every meal (like Ross's mother) tire of the same old mashed or boiled versions.

W

4	POTATOES (PREFERABLY OLD)	4
3	EGG YOLKS	3
1 TBSP	BUTTER, SOFTENED	15 ML
1	EGG YOLK, EXTRA FOR BRUSHING	1

PREHEAT OVEN TO 450° F / 225° C.

*B*oil potatoes until tender; drain and stir over medium heat until very dry. Mash or put through a sieve. Stir in egg yolks and butter; mix well. Cool briefly; put into a piping bag fitted with a star tube. Pipe small swirls onto a greased baking sheet. Brush lightly with extra egg yolk. Bake 10 minutes or until lightly browned.

SERVES 6 TO 8.

New Potatoes Roasted with Garlic

20	BABY NEW POTATOES	20
¼ CUP	VEGETABLE OIL	60 ML
12	CLOVES GARLIC, UNPEELED	12
1 TBSP	ROSEMARY	15 ML

PREHEAT OVEN TO 375° F / 190° C.

Rinse potatoes. Combine all ingredients in a baking dish; mix well. Bake, uncovered, for 45 minutes or until potatoes are well browned and tender. Stir potatoes and garlic twice while roasting. Squeeze the warm garlic from its casing and eat along with the potatoes. Delicious!

SERVES 4.

You may think that this recipe calls for a lot of garlic, but roasted garlic isn't nearly as strong as raw garlic. It's actually sweet. Baby new potatoes are readily available in most supermarkets, but if you have a neighbour who plants potatoes, chances are they won't want the small ones when they're busy with the harvest and will be happy to let you pick up all you like.

W & R

213
CELEBRATING
THE HARVEST

CREAMY SCALLOPED POTATOES

Attend any potluck supper in the Maritimes and you'll find several versions of scalloped potatoes. This is one of those down-home recipes some people argue is better the next day. It's often served with ham, so be sure and put homemade Mustard Pickles on the table as a compliment to both dishes.

W & R

4 OR 5	POTATOES, THINLY SLICED	4 OR 5
¾ CUP	ONIONS, THINLY SLICED	175 ML
2 TBSP	FLOUR, SEASONED WITH SALT AND PEPPER	30 ML
3 TBSP	BUTTER	45 ML
1½ CUPS	MILK, HEATED	375 ML
	DASH OF PAPRIKA	
¼ CUP	CHEDDAR CHEESE, GRATED	50 ML
	PINE NUTS OR SLICED ALMONDS FOR SPRINKLING	

PREHEAT OVEN TO 375° F / 190° C.

Arrange alternate layers of potatoes, onions and seasoned flour in a greased 2-quart / 2-litre casserole. Dot with butter. Pour hot milk over top and sprinkle with paprika. Bake, covered, for 45 minutes. Remove cover and sprinkle with cheese and nuts; bake 15 minutes or until potatoes are tender and top lightly browned.

SERVES 4.

TIP: *To speed up the cooking process, cook the scalloped potatoes in the microwave on high for 10 minutes. This will cut the baking process by about half.*

Potato Latkes

6	POTATOES, PEELED	6
1	SMALL ONION, PEELED	1
½ CUP	ALL-PURPOSE FLOUR	125 ML
1 TBSP	MATZO MEAL OR BREADCRUMBS	15 ML
	SALT AND PEPPER TO TASTE	
2	EGGS, BEATEN	2
2 TBSP	OIL FOR FRYING	30 ML

Grate potatoes into a large bowl filled with cold water and loosely lined with cheesecloth. Lift the cheesecloth to drain potatoes; squeeze briefly to remove starch. Empty water and return potatoes to bowl. Grate onion into potatoes; stir in flour and matzo meal. Season with salt and pepper. Add beaten eggs and mix well.

Heat oil in a large frying pan over medium heat; drop a large dessert spoonful of potato mixture into oil. Spread the mixture out so the latkes will brown nicely on the edges. Sauté 10 minutes; turn over and cook second side 6 minutes.

Serve hot with apple sauce and sour cream.

SERVES 8.

Anyone who listens to CBC Radio's *Morningside* with Peter Gzowski will be familiar with the flamboyant Bessie Selby. Bessie is our local gourmet guru and for several years she had her own TV cooking show in Saint John. She was a guest on our show for a Christmas / Hanukkah special and was kind enough to share this traditional recipe for potato pancakes with us.

W&R

215
CELEBRATING
THE HARVEST

TIP: *If you own a food processor, use it to grate the vegetables. It will speed up the recipe and save your knuckles and your fingernails. If you don't have matzo meal, use breadcrumbs.*

Double-Baked Stuffed Potatoes

My mother told me, "Never mess with what God has already created perfect." Like all kids, I sometimes didn't listen. This potato recipe is decadent enough to even tempt my Mum to ignore her own advice.

R

TIP: *You make a quick lunch or light supper simply by adding hot, cooked broccoli and a bit of chopped ham or chicken to the top of the potato after you take it from the oven.*

6	BAKING POTATOES	6
¼ CUP	BUTTER OR MARGARINE	50 ML
½ CUP	PARMESAN CHEESE	125 ML
⅛ CUP	FRESH PARSLEY OR CHOPPED GREEN ONION	25 ML
1	EGG YOLK	1
⅓ CUP	SOUR CREAM	75 ML
	SALT AND PEPPER TO TASTE	
¼ CUP	CHEDDAR CHEESE, GRATED	50 ML
	DASH OF PAPRIKA	

PREHEAT OVEN TO 425° F / 220° C.

Scrub potatoes, pierce skins with fork, and bake until tender, about 45 minutes. Remove from oven and cool slightly for easier handling.

Cut tops off potato along their length and carefully scoop out contents, reserving potato jackets. In a large pot or bowl, mash potatoes and mix with butter, cheese, parsley or green onion, egg yolk, sour cream, salt and pepper. Fill potato jackets with mashed potato mixture. Top with grated Cheddar and a dash of paprika. Reheat in 350° F / 180° C oven for 20 minutes or until potato is hot and puffy and cheese is melted.

SERVES 6.

Sweet Finale

Cakes, Cookies
and Desserts

1 CUP	WHIPPING CREAM	250 ML
1 TSP	VANILLA EXTRACT	5 ML
	SUGAR TO TASTE	
1	BOX CHOCOLATE WAFERS	1

Whip cream in a chilled bowl. Add vanilla and sugar to taste; continue whipping until cream is stiff.

Spread about ½ inch / 1 cm cream on one side of each chocolate wafer, and sandwich wafers together placing them upright on a rectangular serving tray. When all wafers have been used, spread remaining cream over the log shape, covering all chocolate wafer surfaces. Refrigerate at least 1 hour.

Serve by cutting 1-inch / 2.5-cm slices diagonally to expose black and white stripes. Delicious, easy and oh so elegant!

SERVES 6.

Black Tie Slice

Julie Kate Olivier, daughter of the late Sir Laurence Olivier and actress Joan Plowright, honoured us by spending more than a month at our Inn while rehearsing *Macbeth* under the direction of Tom Kerr. On opening night, Willa suggested we have an après theatre dinner menu to honour our guests. We prepared lobster thermidor, oysters on the half shell, risotto and a very humble dessert we called Black Tie Slice in keeping with the occasion.

R

219
SWEET
FINALE

BLOND BROWNIES

When Mum packed these in our lunches, we became the most popular kids at school. The problem that arises from these squares is whether to eat the topping or the cake first. There is no right way. Some people have even been known to bite into the whole square. This method works best when you have company for tea.

W

½ CUP	BUTTER	125 ML
1 CUP	BROWN SUGAR	250 ML
¾ CUP	ALL-PURPOSE FLOUR	175 ML
¼ TSP	BAKING POWDER	1 ML
½ TSP	SALT	2 ML
¾ CUP	WALNUTS, CHOPPED	175 ML
2	EGGS, LIGHTLY WHIPPED	2
1 TSP	VANILLA EXTRACT	5 ML

FUDGE ICING

1 CUP	BROWN SUGAR	250 ML
¼ CUP	MILK	50 ML
1 Tbsp	BUTTER	15 ML
1 CUP	ICING SUGAR	250 ML
1 TSP	VANILLA EXTRACT	5 ML

Blend butter and brown sugar in a small pot; melt over medium heat, stirring constantly until smooth. (Use your microwave, if you're comfortable doing so. It takes about 1 ½ minutes.) Cool slightly and set aside.

Mix all dry ingredients in a large bowl. Add eggs, vanilla and cooled butter mixture: beat until well blended. Pour into a well-greased 8-inch / 2-litre square pan. Bake 20 to 25 minutes, or until squares spring back when lightly touched. Cool 5 minutes; remove from pan. Set aside.

Mix brown sugar, milk and butter in a saucepan; bring to a boil over medium-high heat. Boil 3 minutes; cool for 5 minutes. Stir in icing sugar and vanilla. Beat until shiny and creamy. If too stiff, add more milk, 1 tsp / 5 ml at a time. Spoon onto cooled squares before mixture cools; spread evenly. Cut into 1-inch / 2.5-cm squares.

MAKES 16 SQUARES.

¼ CUP	BUTTER OR MARGARINE, SOFTENED	50 ML
1 CUP	WHITE SUGAR	250 ML
2	EGGS	2
1 TSP	VANILLA EXTRACT	5 ML
¾ CUP	ALL-PURPOSE FLOUR	175 ML
¼ TSP	SALT	1 ML
⅓ CUP	COCOA	75 ML
2 TBSP	10% CREAM OR WHOLE MILK	30 ML
2 TBSP	WARM WATER	30 ML
¾ CUP	WALNUTS OR PECANS, CHOPPED (OPTIONAL)	175 ML

CHEWY CHOCOLATE BROWNIES

Another of Mum's recipes I've made so many times at the last minute when we've needed a dessert at the Inn. No leavening is used, which makes these brownies lovely and chewy. *W*

PREHEAT OVEN TO 350° F / 180° C.

*B*lend together softened butter and sugar in a mixing bowl. Beat well. Add eggs, still beating, then add vanilla. Measure dry ingredients into a bowl; alternatively add with cream and water to egg mixture. Beat well. Fold in chopped nuts, if desired.

Pour into a greased 8 x 8-inch / 20-cm pan. Bake 30 to 35 minutes.

MAKES 16 SQUARES.

TIP: *For a quick, impressive dessert, cut the still warm brownies into large squares, approximately three across or nine to a pan. Lightly dust a white dish with cocoa, using a sieve. Place a brownie in centre, add a scoop of your favourite ice cream on either side, drizzle with hot chocolate sauce, add a dollop of whipped cream and maraschino cherry, and you've got a sure croud-pleaser.*

Gingerbread

This is one of Mum's original recipes. It's basic, delicious and always turns out great. You can count on it. We serve it often at the Inn and our guests love it.

W

½ CUP	SHORTENING	125 ML
½ CUP	BROWN SUGAR	125 ML
¾ CUP	MOLASSES	175 ML
2	EGGS	2
1¾ CUPS	ALL-PURPOSE FLOUR	425 ML
1½ TSP	BAKING POWDER	7 ML
¾ TSP	BAKING SODA	3 ML
¾ TSP	SALT	3 ML
1½ TSP	GINGER	7 ML
1½ TSP	CINNAMON	7 ML
¼ TSP	CLOVES	1 ML
¾ CUP	BOILING WATER	175 ML
	WHIPPED CREAM AND CINNAMON FOR GARNISHING	

PREHEAT OVEN TO 350° F / 180° C.

Cream shortening and sugar in a large bowl. Add molasses and eggs; beat until light and fluffy. Measure dry ingredients into a separate bowl; add alternately with boiling water to egg mixture. Beat until batter is smooth.

Pour into a well-greased 8-inch / 2-litre square pan; bake for 40 to 45 minutes.

Serve warm with whipped cream, lightly sprinkled with cinnamon.

SERVES 9.

¾ LB	BUTTER, SOFTENED	175 ML
3 CUPS	WHITE SUGAR	750 ML
5	LARGE EGGS	5
1 TSP	VANILLA EXTRACT	5 ML
½ TSP	LEMON JUICE	2 ML
1 TSP	LEMON RIND (ZEST), GRATED	5 ML
3 CUPS	ALL-PURPOSE FLOUR	750 ML
⅞ CUP	GINGER ALE	225 ML

WINNIE'S POUND CAKE

Pound cake is a Maritime favourite, and this one is named after my sister Winnie, who shared her recipe with me. Although it doesn't call for the traditional pound of everything, it is the best pound cake I've ever eaten, and it keeps well for a couple of weeks.

PREHEAT OVEN TO 275° F / 135° C.

Cream butter well in a large bowl, using an electric mixer. Gradually add sugar, creaming thoroughly. Mix in eggs, one at a time, beating well after each addition. Stir in vanilla, lemon juice and zest. Add flour alternately with ginger ale. Beat until smooth.

Pour batter into 2 greased 9 x 5-inch / 2-litre loaf pans and bake for 1 hour; or into a 9 x 4-inch / 3-litre tube pan and bake for 1 ½ hours. Cake should be golden brown and spring back when lightly touched.

Cool in pan for 5 minutes; turn out onto rack to cool completely.

MAKES 2 LOAVES OR 1 LARGE TUBE CAKE.

BLUEBERRY COFFEE CAKE

Coffee cakes are quickly made, they're big enough for a crowd, and they're moist and flavourful just as they are. Serve warm or cold; they're still good!

W&R

¼ CUP	SHORTENING OR VEGETABLE OIL	50 ML
¾ CUP	WHITE SUGAR	175 ML
1	EGG	1
2 CUPS	ALL-PURPOSE FLOUR	500 ML
2 TSP	BAKING POWDER	10 ML
1 TSP	SALT	5 ML
¾ CUP	MILK	175 ML
2 CUPS	FRESH OR FROZEN BLUEBERRIES	500 ML
¾ CUP	BROWN SUGAR	175 ML
1 TSP	CINNAMON	5 ML

PREHEAT OVEN TO 350° F / 180° C.

Cream shortening and sugar in a large bowl or electric stand mixer. Add egg; beat until creamy. Combine flour, baking powder and salt in a separate bowl; add to creamy mixture alternately with milk. Gently stir in blueberries (do not thaw berries if frozen). Pour into a greased 9 x 13-inch / 3.5-litre pan. Mix brown sugar and cinnamon, and sprinkle over batter. Bake for 50 to 55 minutes. Serve warm, as is, or topped with ice cream or blueberry sauce.

SERVES 12.

RHUBARB CAKE

½ CUP	BUTTER OR MARGARINE	125 ML
1 ½ CUPS	WHITE SUGAR	375 ML
1	EGG	1
1 TSP	VANILLA EXTRACT	5 ML
2 CUPS	ALL-PURPOSE FLOUR	500 ML
1 TSP	BAKING SODA	5 ML
1 CUP	BUTTERMILK OR SOUR MILK	250 ML
2 CUPS	RHUBARB (OR MORE)	500 ML
1 TSP	CINNAMON	5 ML
1 CUP	BROWN SUGAR	250 ML
¼ CUP	ALL-PURPOSE FLOUR	50 ML

If you're looking for a coffee cake for a large gathering, try this one.

W & R

PREHEAT OVEN TO 350° F / 180° C.

Cream butter in a large bowl or electric mixer. Add sugar and beat until light and fluffy; mix in egg and vanilla. Blend flour and baking soda in a separate bowl and add to egg mixture alternately with buttermilk. Beat well. Cut rhubarb into 1-inch / 2.5-cm pieces and lightly stir into batter. Spoon into a well-greased 9 x 13-inch / 3.5-litre baking pan. Mix cinnamon, brown sugar and flour, and sprinkle over rhubarb batter. Bake 45 to 55 minutes. Cool 10 minutes on a rack. Cut and serve. If baking with glass, you can cover cake with plastic wrap and store it in the pan.

SERVES 12 TO 18.

225
SWEET FINALE

TIP: *To make sour milk, add 1 tsp lemon juice or cider vinegar to fresh milk, stir and let sit before using.*

Zucchini Cake

There are few undeniable truisms in life. One we've discovered is that there is a certain time each year when everyone has more zucchini squash than they know what to do with. When we realized this, Willa came up with the brilliant idea of devoting an entire show to zucchini. This zucchini cake was a big hit. If you like dark, delicious, moist chocolate cake, and you can lay your hands on a zucchini or two, then this recipe is for you.

R

½ CUP	BUTTER OR MARGARINE, SOFTENED	125 ML
1 ¾ CUPS	SUGAR	425 ML
½ CUP	VEGETABLE OIL	125 ML
2	EGGS, BEATEN	2
1 TSP	VANILLA EXTRACT	5 ML
½ CUP	BUTTERMILK OR SOUR MILK	125 ML
2 ½ CUPS	ALL-PURPOSE FLOUR	625 ML
4 TBSP	COCOA	60 ML
1 TSP	BAKING SODA	5 ML
½ TSP	CINNAMON	2 ML
½ TSP	CLOVES	2 ML
½ TSP	SALT	2 ML
2 CUPS	ZUCCHINI, SHREDDED	500 ML
	ICING SUGAR OR WHIPPED CREAM FOR GARNISHING	

PREHEAT OVEN TO 325° F / 160° C.

Cream butter, sugar and oil in a large bowl. Add eggs, vanilla and buttermilk; mix well. Sift together dry ingredients in a separate bowl. Beat into egg mixture alternately with zucchini.

Spoon into a bundt or tube pan. Bake 40 to 50 minutes. Cool on a rack slightly before removing from pan. Dust with icing sugar before serving, or garnish with whipped cream. Wrapped and refrigerated, this cake will remain moist and will keep for several days.

MAKES 24 SLICES.

Cake

1 ½ CUPS	ALL-PURPOSE FLOUR	375 ML
1 CUP	WHITE SUGAR	250 ML
⅓ CUP	COCOA	75 ML
1 TSP	SALT	5 ML
1 TSP	BAKING SODA	5 ML
1 TSP	BAKING POWDER	5 ML
⅓ CUP	VEGETABLE OIL OR MELTED SHORTENING	75 ML
1 TBSP	WHITE VINEGAR	15 ML
1 TSP	VANILLA EXTRACT	5 ML
1 CUP	WARM WATER	250 ML

Icing

3 TBSP	BUTTER OR MARGARINE, SOFTENED	45 ML
½ TSP	VANILLA EXTRACT	2 ML
	DASH OF SALT	
2 CUPS	ICING SUGAR, SIFTED	500 ML
3 TBSP	COCOA	45 ML
2 ½ TBSP	MILK, WATER OR 10% CREAM	40 ML

Wacky Chocolate Cake

This might well be the first cake your kids ever make. Just the name will inspire them. We guess it's called "wacky" because of the odd variety of ingredients: no eggs or milk, but vinegar and warm water. Anyway, it works, and produces one of the tastiest, moistest, fastest chocolate cakes we've ever made.

W&R

227
SWEET FINALE

PREHEAT OVEN TO 350° F / 180° C.

Mix flour, sugar, cocoa, salt, baking soda and baking powder in a large bowl and make three wells, using the back of a spoon. Pour oil into holes followed by vinegar, vanilla and warm water. Mix well, about 2 minutes by hand or 1 minute with a hand mixer.

Pour into a greased 8-inch / 2-litre square pan. Bake 45 minutes or until top of cake springs back when lightly touched.

COOL 5 MINUTES, THEN TURN ONTO RACK.

To make icing, cream butter with vanilla and salt in a bowl. Mix icing sugar and cocoa and blend into butter mixture alternately with milk, beating until smooth and creamy. Add more icing sugar if too moist or more milk if too stiff. Ice cake when thoroughly cooled.

SERVES 9 TO 16.

Tomato Soup Cake

½ CUP	BUTTER OR MARGARINE	125 ML
1 CUP	WHITE SUGAR	250 ML
10-OZ CAN	TOMATO SOUP	284-ML CAN
1 ½ CUPS	ALL-PURPOSE FLOUR	375 ML
1 TSP	CLOVES	5 ML
1 TSP	CINNAMON	5 ML
1 TSP	NUTMEG	5 ML
¼ TSP	SALT	1 ML
1 TSP	BAKING SODA	5 ML
½ CUP	WALNUTS, CHOPPED	125 ML
1 CUP	RAISINS	250 ML
	ICING SUGAR FOR SPRINKLING	

PREHEAT OVEN TO 350° F / 180° C.

Cream butter and sugar in a large bowl; add tomato soup and beat until light and fluffy. Mix flour, spices, salt and soda in a separate bowl. Slowly blend dry ingredients into soup mixture. Add walnuts and raisins; beat well.

Pour batter into a greased 10-inch / 3-litre pan; bake 35 minutes or until top of cake springs back when lightly touched. Cool in pan 5 minutes; turn out onto rack.

Sprinkle with icing sugar, using a sieve or fine-holed shaker. Cut into squares or slices and serve warm or cold.

SERVES 9 TO 16.

Many readers will likely glance at this recipe and think, "Oh no, a cake with tomato soup in it," and quickly flip to the next recipe. However, a few of you will remember that your mother or grandmother made this delicious, moist cake and served it buttered, as you would a fancy bread. Either way it's truly wonderful, and great for people with egg or dairy allergies. It keeps a long time too, much like a dark fruitcake.

W & R

229
SWEET
FINALE

White Fruitcake

Mum and Dad were married in 1929, exactly six months before the stock market crashed. Dad had his own fish business in the Saint John City Market, and he and Mum rented and furnished a modern apartment. Mum forever bragged about her "blue Moffatt range." This is a recipe from the cookbook she received with the stove. Sadly, the economy collapsed before their first Christmas and they never fully recovered. But we always had our white fruit cake and many precious holiday memories.

W

½ CUP	BUTTER	125 ML
1 CUP	SUGAR	250 ML
3	EGGS	3
1 TSP	VANILLA EXTRACT	5 ML
1 TSP	LEMON EXTRACT	5 ML
½ CUP	MILK	125 ML
2 CUPS	ALL-PURPOSE FLOUR	500 ML
2 TSP	BAKING POWDER	10 ML
½ LB	CANDIED CHERRIES, RED AND GREEN	225 G
¼ LB	CANDIED CITRON, FINELY CUT	115 G
¼ LB	CANDIED PINEAPPLE CHUNKS	115 G
½ LB	COCONUT	225 G
¼ LB	ALMONDS OR PECANS, SLICED OR CHOPPED	115 G
1 LB	WHITE RAISINS	450 G

PREHEAT OVEN TO 300° F / 150° C.

*B*lend butter, sugar, eggs and vanilla and lemon extract in a large bowl with an electric mixer. Sift together flour and baking powder. Add milk and flour mixture alternately to egg mixture, mixing well after each addition. Stir in fruit and nuts; mix until well combined. Pour in a well-greased loaf or tube pan, packing down well.

Bake for 2 to 2 ½ hours or until tester comes out clean. Cool and wrap well in tinfoil and plastic wrap, and keep in a cake tin. If refrigerated, cake will last for several months.

Picnic Lemon Roll

4	EGGS, SEPARATED	4	
¾ CUP	SUGAR	175	ML
3 TBSP	HOT WATER	45	ML
½ TSP	LEMON EXTRACT	2	ML
1 CUP	CAKE OR PASTRY FLOUR	250	ML
1 TSP	BAKING POWDER	5	ML
	PINCH OF CREAM OF TARTAR		
	ICING SUGAR		

There is a nature park and a beach right beside our Inn, and whenever we picnic there, we take along some of this delicious dessert.

W & R

PREHEAT OVEN TO 350° F / 180° C.

Beat egg yolks in a large bowl or electric standing mixer until thick; gradually add half the sugar. Mix at high speed for 3 to 4 minutes while adding the remaining sugar, water and lemon flavouring. Sift flour and baking powder into a separate bowl; add to yolk mixture, beating batter well. Beat egg whites in a separate bowl with cream of tartar until stiff, but not dry. Fold gently into batter. Spread in jelly roll pan lined with greased and waxed paper. Bake 15 to 20 minutes until cake springs back when lightly touched.

Invert pan and remove cake onto clean, dry towel, sprinkled with icing sugar. Carefully remove waxed paper. Roll cake (long way) and let sit. This will help shape the roll. Fill with **Lemon Curd** or your favourite homemade jam; raspberry or strawberry are delicious. Re-roll and sprinkle with icing sugar; cut on an angle and serve warm or cold.

SERVES 8.

231
SWEET,
FINALE

Dark Chocolate Fudge

This is a favourite during the cold winter months. And the kids love to help you. Just be careful when using the microwave; the bowl can get very hot.

R

2 CUPS	MINIATURE MARSHMALLOWS	500 ML
1 LB	SEMI-SWEET REAL CHOCOLATE CHIPS	450 G
11-OZ CAN	SWEETENED CONDENSED MILK	300-ML CAN
1 ½ TSP	VANILLA EXTRACT	7 ML
	PECANS OR WALNUTS FOR GARNISHING	

Combine marshmallows, chips and milk in a 2-quart / 2-litre saucepan. Cook over low heat for 7 to 9 minutes, stirring often, until melted and smooth. Or place ingredients in a glass casserole or glass bowl and microwave on high, stirring after 2 minutes. Continue to cook until melted (approximately 4 minutes, but time varies with each microwave).

Stir until smooth; add vanilla. Pour into a greased 8 or 9-inch / 20 or 22-cm square pan. Refrigerate at least 2 hours or until firm. Cut into small squares.

While the fudge is still warm, top each piece with a half a pecan or walnut or add chopped nuts directly to the hot mixture while you are stirring in the vanilla.

MAKES 2 LBS / 900 G OR 64 SERVINGS.

Old-Fashioned Fudge

3 CUPS	BROWN SUGAR, FIRMLY PACKED	750 ML
3 TBSP	CORN SYRUP	45 ML
1 CUP	MILK	250 ML
	DASH OF SALT	
2 TBSP	BUTTER	30 ML
1 TSP	VANILLA	5 ML
½ CUP	CHOPPED NUTS AND COCONUT (OPTIONAL)	125 ML

Add sugar, syrup, milk and salt to a heavy pan over medium heat. Bring mixture to a boil, stirring constantly until it forms a firm ball in cold water, or reaches 238° F / 115° C on a candy thermometer. Remove from heat.

Add butter and vanilla; beat well, and continue beating until it thickens and is less shiny. If using nuts or coconut, quickly add them at this stage, and pour mixture into a greased 8-inch / 2-litre pan. Score into squares while still warm; cut when cool and firm.

MAKES 16 2-INCH / 5-CM SQUARES.

When we were kids, fudge seemed to loom large in our lives. Mum was always being asked to make fudge for school fund raisers; and because we lived in the country, with few diversions, we also made fudge for fun and entertainment. However, we were always on the look-out for a fudge recipe that never failed. When Connie Buckley gave us this recipe, we stopped looking.

W

233
SWEET
FINALE

TIP: *To make chocolate fudge, just add 1 Tbsp / 15 ml of cocoa to dry ingredients.*

Potato Fudge

One cold Sunday afternoon, Ross and I were reminiscing about our respective childhoods. Despite growing up on opposite coasts, we both had memories of potato fudge. It seemed only right to dig out the ingredients and make a batch.

½ CUP	POTATO, COOKED AND MASHED	125 ML
3 CUPS	COCONUT	750 ML
3 CUPS	ICING SUGAR, SIFTED	750 ML
⅓ CUP	SHORTENING, MELTED	75 ML
2	EGG WHITES, FIRMLY BEATEN	2
¼ CUP	RED GLAZED CHERRIES, CHOPPED	50 ML
	FEW DROPS RED FOOD COLOURING	

Push mashed potato through a sieve and into a large bowl. Add coconut and icing sugar; beat well with an electric mixer. Add shortening and beaten egg whites; beat until well combined.

Press half the mixture over bottom of a buttered 8-inch / 2-litre square pan. Add cherries and colouring to remaining mixture, pressing evenly over white mixture. Refrigerate until set. Store covered in refrigerator up to a week.

MAKES ABOUT 32 SQUARES.

¾ CUP	SHORTENING	175 ML
1 ¼ CUPS	BROWN SUGAR, LIGHTLY PACKED	300 ML
1	EGG	1
2 TBSP	MILK OR 10% CREAM	30 ML
2 TSP	VANILLA EXTRACT	10 ML
1 ½ CUPS	ALL-PURPOSE FLOUR	375 ML
1 TSP	SALT	5 ML
¾ TSP	BAKING SODA	3 ML
1 ½ CUPS	SEMI-SWEET CHOCOLATE CHIPS	375 ML

THE ONE-IS-NEVER-ENOUGH COOKIE

Be warned: these cookies are habit-forming. They are also irresistible to anyone within sniffing range. Always make these cookies when you are alone!

W & R

PREHEAT OVEN TO 375° F / 190° C.

Cream shortening and brown sugar in a large bowl or food processor until light and fluffy. Add egg, milk and vanilla; beat 1 minute by hand or until thoroughly blended. Combine flour, salt and baking soda in a separate bowl. Gradually add to creamed mixture, beating for 1 minute or until well mixed. Stir in chocolate chips.

Drop by heaping teaspoons on an ungreased baking sheet, leaving some space between cookies to allow for spreading while cooking.

Bake 8 to 10 minutes, being careful not to overcook as they should be soft and chewy. Cool 2 minutes and remove to cooling rack. Store in an airtight container and hide until ready to serve.

MAKES ABOUT 3 DOZEN COOKIES.

RAISIN CRISPIES

These should be called "Aunt Mary's cookies" because that's how we've always referred to them. We had her write the recipe for us and sign it. We take these moist, chewy cookies with us on winter walks or ski weekends.

W&R

1 CUP	SEEDLESS RAISINS	250 ML
½ CUP	SHORTENING	125 ML
¼ CUP	WATER	50 ML
¾ CUP	ALL-PURPOSE FLOUR, SIFTED	175 ML
½ TSP	SALT	2 ML
½ TSP	BAKING SODA	2 ML
1 TSP	CINNAMON	5 ML
1 TSP	NUTMEG	5 ML
1 CUP	BROWN SUGAR	250 ML
1 TSP	VANILLA EXTRACT	5 ML
1 ½ CUPS	ROLLED OATS	375 ML

PREHEAT OVEN TO 350° F / 180° C.

Rinse raisins in hot water; drain and set aside. Combine shortening and water in a small pot over medium heat. Heat only until shortening melts, stirring constantly. Cool. Sift dry ingredients in a separate bowl; mix in sugar and add cooled shortening, raisins and vanilla. Blend in oatmeal and stir until well mixed.

Drop by teaspoons onto a greased cookie sheet. Bake 10 minutes, taking care not to overcook. (Cookies should remain soft.) Cool a minute before removing from cookie sheet to wire rack.

MAKES ABOUT 4 DOZEN COOKIES.

1 CUP	BUTTER OR MARGARINE	250 ML
1 ½ CUPS	BROWN SUGAR	375 ML
1	EGG	1
1 ¼ CUPS	OATMEAL	300 ML
1 CUP	COCONUT	250 ML
1 ½ CUPS	ALL-PURPOSE FLOUR	375 ML
1 TSP	CREAM OF TARTAR	5 ML
½ TSP	BAKING SODA	2 ML
¼ TSP	SALT	1 ML

Dad's Cookies

This crispy, buttery cookie was Dad's favourite. Mum always had a tin full in the pantry. They contain no spices but still have a wonderful flavour. Yes, there's oatmeal, but don't try to fool yourself into thinking this is a "healthy" cookie. Not with all that butter!

W

PREHEAT OVEN TO 350° F / 180° C.

Blend butter and sugar in a large bowl; mix by hand or with an electric mixer until smooth and creamy. Add the egg and beat well. Mix dry ingredients in a separate bowl and add them to the egg mixture. Stir until well blended. (Mixture should be quite dry, almost like pastry.) Drop by rounded teaspoons onto a greased cookie sheet. Flatten with a fork.

Bake 10 to 12 minutes or until light golden brown. Cool on a rack and store in air-tight container.

MAKES ABOUT 3 DOZEN COOKIES.

237
SWEET
FINALE

Mum's Molasses Cookies

Molasses was a mainstay in our house, as it was in most Maritime kitchens. We bought it by the gallon or pail and used it with everything. It went on our pancakes at breakfast; it went on bread as an after-school snack; it went in the baked beans at supper. Of course, it went in cookies. And no one made better molasses cookies than Mum.

¼ CUP	BUTTER	50 ML
½ CUP	SHORTENING	125 ML
½ CUP	BROWN SUGAR	125 ML
1 TSP	VANILLA EXTRACT	5 ML
½ CUP	MOLASSES	125 ML
2	EGGS	2
2 CUPS	ALL-PURPOSE FLOUR	500 ML
1 TSP	BAKING SODA	5 ML
1 TSP	SALT	5 ML
½ TSP	CLOVES	2 ML
½ TSP	GINGER	2 ML
1 TSP	CINNAMON	5 ML

PREHEAT OVEN TO 350° F / 180° C.

Combine butter, shortening and sugar in a large bowl; beat with an electric mixer, or by hand, until light and fluffy. Blend in vanilla and molasses. Add eggs and beat again until fluffy. Stir together dry ingredients in a separate bowl to combine thoroughly. Gradually stir dry ingredients into butter mixture, beating until well combined.

Drop by large teaspoons onto a well-greased cookie sheet, about 2 inches / 5 cm apart. Bake 10 to 12 minutes. Cookies should be soft and moist. Cool on a rack.

MAKES ABOUT 3 DOZEN COOKIES.

Scotch Cakes

½ LB	BUTTER	225 G
½ CUP	BROWN SUGAR	125 ML
2 CUPS	FLOUR	500 ML

Chocolate Almond Glaze (optional)

½ CUP	SEMI-SWEET CHOCOLATE CHIPS	125 ML
2 TSP	VEGETABLE OIL	10 ML
½ CUP	ALMONDS, FINELY CHOPPED	125 ML

PREHEAT OVEN TO 350° F / 180° C.

Blend butter, sugar and flour thoroughly, either by hand or in a food processor, until mixture leaves sides of bowl and forms a ball. With floured fingers, press dough evenly on bottom of a greased 8-inch / 20-cm pan. Score dough into 16 squares; score each square into two triangles. Prick each triangle twice with a fork. Bake in a preheated oven 25 minutes or until set and edges are very lightly browned. Cool 5 minutes. Cut into triangles; cool completely in pan. Serve plain or ice with a light almond icing; decorate with red and green cherries or dip in chocolate almond sauce.

To make chocolate almond sauce: Combine chips and oil in a saucepan. Cook over medium-litreow heat for 4 to 5 minutes, stirring constantly until chocolate is melted, or melt in microwave for 3 to 4 minutes, stirring occasionally. Remove from heat. Dip one cut edge of each triangle ¼ inch / 5 mm into melted chocolate; scrape against side of pan to remove excess chocolate. Dip chocolate-coated edge into chopped almonds; place on wire rack. Let stand until chocolate is firm.

MAKES 32 TRIANGLES.

Nana's Original Scotch Cakes

What recipe could be easier or faster than one with three ingredients that you put in a square pan, bake, cut and serve? Or one that will last for weeks, can be made into cookies, and is delicious even without fancy icing or decoration? My mother's Scotch cakes. Ask anyone in the family and they'll tell you these cakes meant Christmas at our house. They still do.

W

Butter Tarts

This is one of the first sweets to disappear from any reception. Make them small so that everyone can have at least one – although one is never enough. To serve butter tarts as a dessert, simply make them larger and serve them with a "dollop" of whipped cream topped with a walnut or pecan.

W & R

TIP: A nice variation, popular in the Maritimes, substitutes ½ cup / 125 ml raisins or currants for the nuts. Pour boiling water over the raisins or currants and soak them while you prepare the filling, then drain thoroughly and fold them into the batter.

PASTRY FOR TART SHELLS

¼ CUP	BUTTER OR MARGARINE, SOFTENED	50 ML
½ CUP	BROWN SUGAR, LIGHTLY PACKED	125 ML
1	EGG	1
½ TSP	VANILLA EXTRACT	2 ML
½ TSP	LEMON JUICE	2 ML
½ CUP	CORN SYRUP	125 ML
¼ TSP	SALT	1 ML
½ CUP	WALNUTS OR PECANS, CHOPPED	125 ML

PREHEAT OVEN TO 375° F / 190° C.

To make tart shells, first prepare **Pastry** and roll out, one ball at a time. Cut into 4-inch / 10-cm rounds. Ease gently into tart tin, fluting edges.

Cream butter and sugar in a mixing bowl. Beat in egg, vanilla and lemon juice; blend in corn syrup and salt. Add chopped nuts and spoon into prepared 3-inch / 8-cm tart shells.

Bake 20 minutes or until pastry is golden and filling set. Remove from tins and cool on racks.

MAKES ABOUT 2 DOZEN TARTS.

4	LARGE BAKING APPLES	4
	(CORTLANDS OR GRAVENSTEINS)	
½ CUP	CRANBERRY SAUCE	125 ML
2 TBSP	BROWN SUGAR	30 ML
1 TBSP	BUTTER	15 ML
¾ CUP	BOILING WATER	175 ML

PREHEAT OVEN TO 350° F / 180° C.

Core apples to within ½ inch / 1 cm of bottom; fill centres with **Cranberry Sauce** and equal amounts of sugar. Dot tops with butter. Place in a 8-inch / 20-cm square ovenproof pan with boiling water. Bake 30 to 45 minutes or until tender, being careful not to overcook, as they will burst their skins and fall apart. Serve hot or cold with whipped cream, ice cream or simply as they are.

SERVES 4.

BAKED APPLES WITH CRANBERRY FILLING

Everyone loves baked apples. They're quick and healthy, and with the skins off they can be fed to toddlers.

W&R

241
SWEET FINALE

TIP: *This dessert can also be cooked entirely in the microwave. Cook, covered, in small individual bowls or a glass baking dish on medium-high (70% power) until tender (13 to 14 minutes); turn apples halfway through cooking. Let stand, covered, for 5 minutes.*

CRANAPPLE CRISP

The combination of apples and cranberries is a marriage made in heaven. Both fruits are abundant in the fall; their flavours are complementary, and they offer great eye appeal. Should you like your crisp with apples only, no problem: save the cranberries for the turkey.

W & R

1 CUP	FLOUR	250 ML
1 CUP	ROLLED OATS	250 ML
1 CUP	BROWN SUGAR	250 ML
½ CUP	BUTTER OR MARGARINE	125 ML
1 TSP	CINNAMON	5 ML
½ TSP	NUTMEG	2 ML
3 CUPS	CHOPPED APPLE	750 ML
1 CUP	CRANBERRIES	250 ML
1 TBSP	BUTTER	15 ML

PREHEAT OVEN TO 350° F / 180° C.

Mix together flour, rolled oats and half the brown sugar in a large bowl. Cut in butter with a knife or pastry blender. Combine cinnamon and nutmeg with remaining sugar in a small bowl. Mix apple and cranberries in a large bowl; stir in the spiced sugar mixture. Mix one-quarter of crumb mix into apple and cranberries. Spread one-quarter of the crumb mixture in the bottom of a well-buttered baking dish or small casserole. Add mixed fruit and dot with butter. Cover with remaining crumbs. Pat down slightly. Bake for 30 minutes. Serve alone or with maple ice cream.

SERVES 6.

TIP: *Do you have an abundance of rhubarb? Make rhubarb crisp using the same recipe. Just leave out the cranberries and nutmeg.*

Apple-Raisin Squares

2 CUPS	ALL-PURPOSE FLOUR	500 ML
¼ CUP	SUGAR	50 ML
¼ TSP	SALT	1 ML
½ CUP	BUTTER OR MARGARINE	125 ML
3 TBSP	BUTTER	45 ML
2 LBS	APPLES, PEELED AND CORED	900 G
½ CUP	SEEDLESS RAISINS	125 ML
⅓ CUP	LIGHT BROWN SUGAR	75 ML
½ TSP	CINNAMON	2 ML
1 TBSP	CORNSTARCH	15 ML
2 TBSP	LEMON JUICE	30 ML
¾ CUP	ALL-PURPOSE FLOUR	175 ML
¾ CUP	PECANS, CHOPPED	175 ML
⅓ CUP	LIGHT BROWN SUGAR	75 ML
6 TBSP	BUTTER, SOFTENED	90 ML
2 TSP	VANILLA EXTRACT	10 ML
¾ TSP	CINNAMON	3 ML

Although we hate to see summer end, we do look forward to the fresh apples of autumn. With so many apple growers scattered throughout the countryside, we get the freshest fruit at reasonable prices. Pair this up with a weekend drive and perhaps one of the last picnics of the year, followed by this rich, streusel-litreike square, and you and your family will be glad it's October.

W & R

243
SWEET
FINALE

PREHEAT OVEN TO 375° F / 180° C.

Blend flour, sugar and salt in a large bowl. With pastry blender or two knives, cut in ½ cup/125 ml butter until mixture resembles fine crumbs; press evenly onto bottom of a lightly greased 9 x 13-inch / 3.5-litre baking pan. Bake crust for 15 to 20 minutes until golden. Don't be upset if crust cracks slightly. Remove to rack from oven.

Melt 3 Tbsp butter in a large frying pan over medium heat. Cut apples into ½-inch / 1-cm pieces and add to melted butter along with raisins, brown sugar and cinnamon. Cook 15 minutes, stirring occasionally, until apples are tender. Mix cornstarch and lemon juice in a cup; stir into apple mixture until thick (which will happen immediately); remove from heat. Spoon apple mixture over crust.

Mix together flour, pecans, brown sugar, butter, vanilla and cinnamon in a bowl.

Spread pecan mixture over apple mixture, and bake a further 30 minutes or until topping is browned. Cool completely in pan on a wire rack. When cold, cut into three strips, lengthwise, then cut each strip into 12 pieces.

MAKES 36 SQUARES.

Blueberry Grunt

1 CUP	ALL-PURPOSE FLOUR	250 ML
1 TBSP	SUGAR	15 ML
2 TSP	BAKING POWDER	10 ML
¼ TSP	SALT	1 ML
3 TBSP	SHORTENING OR VEGETABLE OIL	45 ML
1	EGG, BEATEN	1
⅓ CUP	MILK	75 ML
2 ½ CUPS	BLUEBERRIES, FRESH OR FROZEN	625 ML
½ CUP	SUGAR	125 ML
2 TBSP	FLOUR	30 ML
¾ CUP	FRUIT JUICE (APPLE, ORANGE OR LEMON) OR WATER	175 ML
1 TBSP	BUTTER OR MARGARINE	15 ML

No Maritime cookbook would be complete without blueberry grunt or cobbler, as it is more commonly known.

W & R

PREHEAT OVEN TO 375° F / 190° C.

Sift together 1 cup flour, 1 Tbsp sugar, baking powder and salt; cut or blend in shortening. Add egg and milk. Stir with a fork to make a moist drop batter. Set aside.

Rinse blueberries, removing any stems or leaves. Place in a bowl with sugar; set aside. Blend together flour and juice in a saucepan. Cook over medium heat until mixture comes to a boil, stirring constantly. Add berries; continue cooking over low heat until berries are tender, about 10 minutes.

Pour hot mixture into an 8-inch / 2-litre casserole; dot with butter. Top with biscuit dough, dropping it with a tablespoon onto hot blueberries. Do not stir. Bake 35 to 40 minutes until biscuits are brown. Serve hot with vanilla ice cream.

SERVES 6.

Blueberry Topping

This topping is delicious in combination with **Dessert Crêpes** or over vanilla ice cream. Make some in advance; it will keep in the refrigerator for a week or more.

W&R

1 Tbsp	BUTTER	15 ML
3 Tbsp	SUGAR	45 ML
½ Cup	BLUEBERRIES	125 ML
1 Tsp	CORNSTARCH	5 ML
2 Tbsp	APPLE JUICE OR WATER	30 ML
1 Tbsp	ORANGE OR ALMOND LIQUEUR	15 ML

Melt butter and sugar in a small saucepan over medium heat. Add frozen or fresh blueberries; cook for 3 or 4 minutes until sauce takes on colour of berries. Mix cornstarch with apple juice or water in a separate cup or bowl. Add to berry sauce; stir well. Continue to cook about 1 minute. Add orange or almond liqueur, if you wish.

If using on **Dessert Crêpes**, place small spoonful of ice cream on each crêpe and add a few fresh berries. Roll crêpe and pour warm sauce over it. Serve on a dessert plate with a sprig of mint.

MAKES 1½ CUPS / 375 ML.

PUMPKIN CHIFFON DESSERT

1 TBSP	UNFLAVOURED GELATIN	15 ML
¼ CUP	WATER	50 ML
½ CUP	BROWN SUGAR, LIGHTLY PACKED	125 ML
1 TSP	CINNAMON	5 ML
½ TSP	GINGER	2 ML
¼ TSP	CLOVES	1 ML
¼ TSP	ALLSPICE	1 ML
½ TSP	SALT	2 ML
1 ½ CUPS	PURÉED PUMPKIN, FRESH, CANNED OR FROZEN	375 ML
3	EGGS, SEPARATED	3
½ CUP	MILK	125 ML
¼ CUP	BROWN SUGAR, LIGHTLY PACKED	50 ML

We grow the world's biggest pumpkins here in the Maritimes, but it's the smaller ones that produce the sweetest flavour. Although they store well in a dry, cool place, we find it easier to peel, cook and purée our pumpkin, and freeze it for future recipes.

W&R

Mix gelatin and water in a cup or small bowl. Combine ½ cup / 125 ml brown sugar, spices, and salt in the top of a double boiler; add pumpkin, egg yolks and milk. Beat until smooth. Cook over boiling water about 10 minutes until thick and smooth, stirring constantly. Remove from heat and blend in gelatin liquid. Pour into a bowl and chill until mixture moulds slightly, stirring occasionally. (This requires about 1 hour in the refrigerator or about half an hour if the bowl is set in a pan of ice water.)

Beat egg whites to soft peaks, gradually beating in ¼ cup / 50 ml brown sugar. Fold meringue into chilled pumpkin mixture. Generously fill parfait or champagne glasses or one baked pie shell. Chill in refrigerator for 2 to 3 hours or until firm. Serve cold, plain or topped with whipped cream.

SERVES 8 TO 10.

PASTRY

Mum made all the pastry when I lived at home, and she did it all from "feel." It did me no good to ask her how much of anything to use. Her response was generally, "Oh, you know, until it feels right." That was then. Now I know. But in between, I read everything I could get my hands on that had to do with making pastry. Only recently I discovered I could make it in our food processor. Wow! That machine has a real sense of feel; it makes great pastry.

W

2 CUPS	ALL-PURPOSE FLOUR	500 ML
1 TSP	SALT	5 ML
1 CUP	SHORTENING	250 ML
¼ CUP	COLD WATER	50 ML

Blend or sift together dry ingredients in a large bowl. Using a pastry blender or two knives, cut in shortening. When mixture is the size of peas, sprinkle with cold water, a little at a time, mixing lightly with a fork until all the flour is dampened. (Or use your food processor, pulsing the mixture until it comes away from the side of the bowl.) Turn dough onto a piece of waxed paper and form into a ball. Chill if desired.

To roll, use a lightly floured surface. Divide pastry in two and form each half into a flattened ball. Roll lightly, from the centre to the edge each time, until the pastry is just slightly larger than the inverted pie plate.

To line pie plate, fold rolled pastry in half and transfer it to the plate, or roll over the rolling pin and gently roll onto the plate. Trim off any extra pastry with scissors or a sharp knife.

For individual meat pies, roll out pastry, invert the pot on the dough, and trim around the pot with a knife, being sure to make the crust slightly bigger than the pot.

Makes 1 9-inch / 23-cm double crust pie; 2 9-inch / 23-cm shells, or 24 small tart shells.

To cook, follow directions for recipes requiring pastry.

RASPBERRY PIE

	PASTRY FOR 1 PIE SHELL	
4 CUPS	RASPBERRIES	1 L
1 CUP	SUGAR (OR LESS)	250 ML
3 TBSP	FLOUR	45 ML
⅛ TSP	SALT	.5 ML
1 TBSP	BUTTER OR MARGARINE	15 ML

PREHEAT OVEN TO 400° F / 200° C.

PREPARE PASTRY.

Line a 9-inch / 23-cm pie plate with rolled pastry. Roll out pastry for top and cut into strips for lattice top.

Prepare raspberries by washing and draining, being careful to remove stems and leaves. Combine sugar, flour and salt in a separate bowl. Place half of the berries in pie shell. Add half of the sugar mixture. Add remaining berries and sugar mixture to the pie shell. Dot with pieces of butter.

Arrange pastry strips on top of pie, lattice fashion, so strips go over, then under, the next strip. Moisten, seal at edge and where strips cross. Trim and flute edges.

Bake 40 to 50 minutes, or until pastry is golden brown. Cool slightly and serve as is, or top with ice cream.

MAKES 1 PIE. SERVES 6 TO 8.

As children we loved summer, but we had mixed feelings about August and raspberry season. Dad had several rows of raspberries and we had to beat our way through the prickles to fill pint boxes to sell at local markets. It was years before I could enjoy any dish made with raspberries! Now, raspberry pie is part of our summer tradition. We generally try to freeze a few bags of berries so we can xperience that August feeling in the dead of winter. We're still picking from the same patch Dad planted 45 years ago.

W

249
SWEET
FINALE

Tip: If using frozen, unsweetened berries, partially thaw and drain before using. If using presweetened frozen berries, reduce sugar to ¼ cup / 50 ml.

Glazed Strawberry Pie

4 CUPS	STRAWBERRIES, HULLED	1 L
1	9-INCH / 2.5-LITRE PIE SHELL, BAKED	1
¾ CUP	SUGAR	175 ML
2 TBSP	CORNSTARCH	30 ML
½ CUP	WATER	125 ML
1 TBSP	LEMON JUICE	15 ML
	WHIPPED CREAM FOR GARNISHING	

For many years we had our own strawberry patch. The year I discovered this recipe, I stopped making shortcakes and made fourteen strawberry pies. For the crew at CBC Radio, Saint John, where I was a freelance writer-broadcaster, I made tarts, which we consumed at seven in the morning. Although I've never again made fourteen strawberry pies in one season, this pie has become a favourite with our guests at the Inn.

W

Rinse and dry berries thoroughly. Arrange 3 cups / 750 ml perfect berries close together, with points up, in pie shell. Mash remaining berries in a small saucepan and stir in a mixture of sugar, cornstarch and water. Cook, stirring over low heat, until thick and clear. Remove from heat; add lemon juice. Stir until slightly cooled, and spoon over berries. Chill pie thoroughly. Garnish with whipped cream.

MAKES 1 PIE. SERVES 6 TO 8.

250
SWEET
FINALE

2	EGGS	2
13 OZ	EVAPORATED MILK	385 ML
2 CUPS	MAPLE SYRUP	500 ML
1 ½ TBSP	ALL-PURPOSE FLOUR	25 ML
2	UNBAKED PIE SHELLS	2

PREHEAT OVEN TO 400° F / 200° C.

Beat eggs and evaporated milk well in a large bowl, gradually adding maple syrup and flour. Pour into pie shells. Bake for about 45 minutes or until knife inserted into filling comes out clean, but not dry. Serve with whipped cream or ice cream.

  A great tasting dessert. Thank you, Suzanne!

MAKES 2 PIES.

Maple Syrup Pie

This recipe was given to me when I visited the Cabane à Sucre Pigeon behind Poley Mountain in Sussex, New Brunswick. Gaetan and Suzanne Pigeon kindly let us tape a *Tide's Table* program right in their sugar bush. It was early April, the bright sunshine was melting the snow, and the sap was running strong. Suzanne Pigeon insisted I try a piece of her maple syrup pie before leaving, and she carefully wrote out this recipe. We halved the recipe and baked one pie with little trouble.

R

Mocha Mousse

Always a classic, mousse is a nice, light dessert to top off any meal, particularly if it has been preceded by several heavy courses.

W & R

¾ CUP	CRUSHED ICE, DRAINED	175 ML
2 TBSP	COLD WATER	30 ML
1	ENVELOPE UNFLAVOURED GELATIN	7 G
2 TBSP	INSTANT COFFEE GRANULES	30 ML
½ CUP	BOILING WATER	125 ML
⅔ CUP	SEMI-SWEET CHOCOLATE CHIPS	150 ML
1 TBSP	SUGAR	15 ML
¼ TSP	VANILLA OR COFFEE LIQUEUR	1 ML
½ CUP	WHIPPING CREAM	125 ML

Crush ice in blender and set aside in refrigerator. Pour cold water into blender jar and add gelatin; let set 15 to 20 seconds. Add coffee granules and boiling water. Cover and blend until gelatin is dissolved, about 1 minute. Add chocolate chips, sugar and liqueur. Blend at Liquefy until mixture is smooth, about 1 minute. Pour in crushed ice and cream. Blend at Liquefy, pulsing 3 to 4 times, about 10 seconds each time, until mixture begins to thicken. Pour into dessert dishes. Refrigerate about 20 to 30 minutes until set.

SERVES 4.

½ TSP	ORANGE RIND (ZEST), GRATED	2 ML
2 TBSP	LIGHT BROWN SUGAR	30 ML
1	EGG YOLK	1
1	EGG	1
3 OZ	SEMI-SWEET CHOCOLATE	90 G
1 TBSP	ORANGE LIQUEUR OR ORANGE JUICE	15 ML
½ TBSP	ORANGE JUICE	7 ML
½ CUP	WHIPPING CREAM	125 ML
	WHIPPED CREAM AND ORANGE RIND (ZEST) FOR GARNISHING	

CHOCOLATE-ORANGE MOUSSE

If you assemble your ingredients first, as you should always do, this recipe will only take about five minutes to make. It will look like chocolate milk when you pour it into the dishes, but don't despair. It will thicken to the consistency of a creamy truffle.

W&R

Combine orange zest, brown sugar, egg yolk and egg in a blender or food processor. Blend until light and foamy. Melt chocolate in a small saucepan over low heat. Cool for a few minutes. Drizzle into blender along with orange liqueur, orange juice and cream. Blend until well mixed.

Pour into parfait glasses or long-stemmed wine glasses. Refrigerate for at least 1 hour or until ready to use. Garnish with whipped cream and a twist of orange rind.

SERVES 2.

253
SWEET
FINALE

Blueberry Ballerina

I created this variation of the famous Pavlova, named for Russian ballerina Anna Pavlova. That dish originally hailed from Australia and used strawberries and kiwi fruit. This Maritime version of the dessert is equally spectacular, but surprisingly easy to prepare.

R

Tip: A meringue dessert like this is best made when the weather is dry.

4 TO 6	EGG WHITES, AT ROOM TEMPERATURE	4 TO 6
1 CUP	WHITE SUGAR	250 ML
1 TBSP	CORNSTARCH	15 ML
	PINCH CREAM OF TARTAR	
	PINCH OF SALT	
1 TSP	VANILLA EXTRACT	5 ML
2 TSP	CIDER VINEGAR	10 ML
	FRESHLY WHIPPED CREAM	
1 ½ CUPS	FRESH BLUEBERRIES	375 ML

PREHEAT OVEN TO 400° F / 200° C.

Beat egg whites with an electric mixer, gradually adding sugar. Continue to beat until whites are very stiff. Fold in cornstarch, cream of tartar and salt. Mix in vanilla and vinegar. Place a double layer of wet waxed paper on a baking sheet. (We wrinkle our waxed paper and place it directly under the water tap.) Pile meringue in a circle with the sides slightly higher than centre. Place in preheated oven and turn it off. Let stand for 1½ hours.

Remove meringue from oven and carefully separate from waxed paper. (Don't let it stand too long or the job will be more difficult). Pieces of the meringue will break off, but don't panic; just put them back, or ignore them. Pile meringue with sweetened whipped cream and fresh blueberries for serving at the family table, or place individual servings on white dessert plates, and surround with a blueberry coulis or blueberry sauce.

SERVES 8.

1 CUP	WATER	250 ML
¾ CUP	WHITE SUGAR	175 ML
2	SPRIGS FRESH ROSEMARY	2
6 CUPS	RHUBARB, CHOPPED	1.5 L
½ CUP	WATER	125 ML
2 TBSP	LEMON JUICE	30 ML
	PINCH OF SALT	
1	ENVELOPE UNFLAVOURED GELATIN	1
1	EGG WHITE	1
	ROSEMARY LEAVES OR LEMON ZEST	
	FOR GARNISHING	

RHUBARB & ROSEMARY SORBET

Sorbets are one of those "guests" that, once they stay over, become an important part of one's recipe repertoire. These delicious, icy palate pleasers can be a tangy dessert after a full rich meal. Their sweet-sour tartness is also the perfect tastebud refresher between courses. Sorbets allow your mouth to experience the delicate flavour of a salmon entrée after consuming a biting garlic-dressed salad. Here's a unique one we use regularly.

R

255
SWEET
FINALE

Bring 1 cup / 250 ml water, sugar and fresh rosemary to boil in a stainless steel pot over medium heat, stirring frequently. Simmer 5 minutes; remove from heat. Let stand another 15 minutes and strain. Reserve sugar syrup. Wash rhubarb and chop into 1-inch / 2.5-cm chunks. Place in a stainless steel pot with water, lemon juice and salt. Bring to a boil over medium heat; simmer for 5 minutes. Remove from heat, stir in sugar syrup; sprinkle gelatin powder over mixture. Mix well and cool. Beat egg white until soft peaks form. Fold into rhubarb mixture; place in freezer for 1 to 2 hours until almost firm. Remove and beat well with electric mixer or process in food processor until smooth and creamy. Freeze in a covered container for 2 or 3 hours or until set .

Soften at room temperature about 20 minutes before serving. To serve, use a small ice cream scoop; scrape a walnut-sized ball from the surface of the frozen sorbet. Decorate with fresh rosemary leaves or lemon zest and serve as a palate refresher between courses.

MAKES ABOUT 6 CUPS. SERVES 36.

Raspberry Vinegar Sorbet

I will always remember the raspberry vinegar drink served by my grandmother on the hot summer days of my youth. The piquant vinegar aroma mixed with the sweet flavour of fresh raspberry juice that was chilled to icy temperatures in the old chest refrigerator on Grandma's back porch. That memory spawned raspberry vinegar sorbet at the Inn. It's wonderful as a light dessert or palate refresher.

R

4 CUPS	FRESH RASPBERRIES	1 L
1 CUP	WATER	250 ML
¾ CUP	WHITE SUGAR	175 ML
1 TBSP	LEMON JUICE	15 ML
1	ENVELOPE UNFLAVOURED GELATIN	1
3 TBSP	CIDER VINEGAR	45 ML
	LEMON ZEST OR FRESH MINT LEAVES	
	FOR GARNISHING	

Place raspberries, water, sugar and lemon juice into a stainless steel pan over medium heat. Bring to a boil, then simmer, stirring frequently for about 5 minutes, until sugar is completely dissolved and berries are softened. Press raspberry mixture through a sieve; discard pulp and seeds. In the same pan, sprinkle gelatin over raspberry syrup; let stand 5 minutes. Mix well and reheat, if necessary, until gelatin is completely dissolved. Remove from heat; add cider vinegar and stir to mix. Place in a steel bowl in freezer for 1 to 2 hours, until partially firm. Remove and beat well with electric mixer, or place in blender until smooth and creamy. Freeze, covered, for 2 or 3 hours, or until set.

Before serving, soften the sorbet at room temperature for 20 minutes. To serve, use a small ice-cream scoop, and scrape a small ball from the surface of the frozen sorbet. Place in a delicate dessert dish and accent with lemon zest or fresh mint leaves.

MAKES ABOUT 5 CUPS. SERVES 30.

1	GRAPEFRUIT	1	
¼ CUP	LIME JUICE	50 ML	
	WATER, AS NEEDED		
⅔ CUP	WHITE SUGAR	150 ML	
1	ENVELOPE UNFLAVOURED GELATIN	1	
¼ CUP	WATER	50 ML	
¼ CUP	TEQUILA	50 ML	
1 TBSP	LIME OR LEMON RIND (ZEST), GRATED	15 ML	

Cut grapefruit in half. Using a sharp knife or spoon, remove grapefruit flesh or segments, and place in a glass measuring cup. Add lime juice and enough water to make 2 cups / 500 ml. Combine with sugar in a stainless steel pot over medium heat; stir until sugar is dissolved. Simmer for 15 minutes. Sprinkle gelatin powder into ¼ cup / 50 ml water. Let stand 5 minutes until dissolved. Add to grapefruit mixture and remove from heat. Mix well. Add tequila and lime zest. Process in blender or food processor until smooth. Pour into a metal bowl, cover and freeze 1½ or 2 hours until just set. Beat with an electric mixer until somewhat smooth and frothy. Cover and freeze again until firm. Before serving, remove from freezer and soften at room temperature for about 20 minutes. Scrape into walnut size balls and serve as a palate refresher.

MAKES ABOUT 4 CUPS. SERVES 24.

Tequila Sorbet

When vacationing in Mexico, we did the "tourista" thing and returned with a giant bottle of tequila. Now what to do with it? We imbibe moderately at most. We put this prickly potion to use by including it in our lime and grapefruit sorbet. Serve with a flourish and shout "Olé."

W&R

257
SWEET
FINALE

Plum Pudding

We are traditionalists, especially at Christmas. As soon as the "kids" arrive home in late December, we get a real tree and we help them trim it. We all drink eggnog and "ooh" and "aah" over the handmade decorations brought home from nursery schools years ago. We lovingly unwrap the antique birds and balls from Nana and Poppy's tree. We all open one gift (if we want to) on Christmas Eve, and we all eat too much on Christmas day, including plum pudding with hard sauce and lemon sauce.

W & R

DRY INGREDIENTS

½ LOAF	DAY-OLD BREAD, CRUMBED	½ LOAF
¼ LB	GROUND SUET	50 ML
1 CUP	ALL-PURPOSE FLOUR	250 ML
¼ CUP	BROWN SUGAR	50 ML
½ CUP	APPLE, PEELED AND CHOPPED	125 ML
½ CUP	RAISINS	125 ML
¾ CUP	CURRANTS	175 ML
3	CANDIED PINEAPPLE RINGS, CHOPPED	3
⅓ CUP	GLAZED CHERRIES, CHOPPED	75 ML
⅓ CUP	PECANS, CHOPPED	75 ML
¼ CUP	ALMONDS, FLAKED	50 ML
1 TBSP	CINNAMON	15 ML
1 TSP	GINGER	5 ML
½ TSP	ALLSPICE	2 ML
¼ TSP	NUTMEG	1 ML
⅛ TSP	SALT	.5 ML

WET INGREDIENTS

2	EGGS	2
1 TBSP	LEMON JUICE	15 ML
¼ CUP	ORANGE JUICE	50 ML
1	LEMON RIND (ZEST), GRATED	1
¼ CUP	RUM	50 ML
¼ CUP	SHERRY	50 ML
⅛ CUP	WHIPPING CREAM	25 ML

*M*ix together the dry ingredients in a large bowl. Beat together the wet ingredients in a separate bowl. Blend together the dry and wet ingredients until well mixed. If batter needs more moisture, add extra rum. Pour into a well-greased 6-cup / 1.5-litre mould or metal bowl. Place a double layer of greased waxed paper on top, and cover with a double layer of aluminum foil. Tie tightly with heavy string. Place rack in a Dutch oven or large pan; add 2 inches / 5 cm of boiling water. Place mould on rack. Bring water to a full boil; cover with lid. Reduce heat to low and simmer for 2 ½ hours or until centre of pudding springs back when lightly touched. Remove from Dutch oven; cool 3 to 5 minutes. Wrap well and store until Christmas.

To reheat, wrap in aluminum foil and bake at 350° F / 180° C for 30 to 40 minutes or steam as before for 30 to 40 minutes until heated through and serve with **Hard Sauce** and/or **Lemon Sauce**.

HARD SAUCE

⅓ CUP	BUTTER, SOFTENED	75 ML
1 CUP	ICING SUGAR, SIFTED	250 ML
1 TBSP	RUM, SHERRY OR BRANDY	15 ML
	OR	
1 TSP	VANILLA	5 ML

*C*ream butter in a small bowl, gradually adding icing sugar. Beat until creamy. Blend in chosen flavouring and beat well.

Place in a serving dish and chill thoroughly, or fill a pastry tube and pipe rosettes to place around plum pudding.

MAKES 1 CUP.

LEMON SAUCE

½ CUP	SUGAR	125 ML
3 TBSP	FLOUR	45 ML
1 TSP	LEMON RIND (ZEST), GRATED	5 ML
¼ TSP	SALT	1 ML
1 ¼ CUPS	BOILING WATER	300 ML
3 TBSP	LEMON JUICE	45 ML
2 TBSP	BUTTER	30 ML

Combine sugar, flour, zest and salt in a small saucepan. Slowly stir in boiling water. Cook, stirring constantly, over medium heat for 5 to 7 minutes until sauce is thick. Blend in lemon juice and butter.

Serve hot over steamed plum pudding with hard sauce on the side.

MAKES 1½ CUPS.

INDEX